A Love of Being

A Love of Being

My Mother's Daughter

NancyAnn Darr

Library of Congress Control Number:		2010903854
ISBN:	Hardcover	978-1-4500-6437-8
	Softcover	978-1-4500-6436-1
	Ebook	978-1-4500-6438-5

This book was printed in the United States of America.

To order additional copies of this book, contact:
Xlibris Corporation
1-888-795-4274
www.Xlibris.com
Orders@Xlibris.com
78042

I would like to dedicate this book to all my family and extended family, and to all of the descendents of my wonderful mother, Thelma Gaw. We are all grateful for her influence in our lives. I am also thankful to have all of you in my life.

With my love, NancyAnn Darr

For my Aunt Grace,
You have been a wonderful
part of my life. I also
feel we are alike in
many ways. I Love You!
NancyAnn

There has been a lot written on the subject of Mother and child relationships, which is highly evident especially in the month of May as you peruse the magazine covers prior to Mothers' Day. It's a subject that is non-ending, and I feel the most important of family relationships. The many facets of a mother-child relationship are so great that I will not delve into all those, even though you will find many examples throughout the story of my life and my mother's role in those adventures. My focus in these writings is based on the strong role my mother played in my life and the memories she gave me, and my memories that she related to me regarding her childhood. My hope is to convey to my family what their grandmother and "Gigi" was all about, and instill in them wonderful memories that will last forever and be passed on to their descendents. All that knew Gigi already have wonderful and loving memories of her but I hope I can add to their present ones. I want to impart how her life intertwined mine as I grew up, and how her role as a best friend played out. I hope it will also give my children and grandchildren an understanding of what my life was like and how other people play such an important role in your life and what joy they can bring.

In a biography such as this, it is almost impossible to include all events that occurred. However, I would like to tell you about some of the most memorable ones. I will not be including lots of dates, as I don't feel that is the significant part. I will relate happenings in a sequential order that I hope will be clear and create a picture of history in a familial way.

The name of this book in no way is to insinuate my love for my dad was lesser than that for my mom, because it was not. My mother, however, had a very special connection and one that was very close and meaningful, therefore the title.

Theodore holding Thelma Florence with Inez

Thelma at 22

Thelma Etta Fugate was born with green eyes and strawberry blonde hair, on August 30th, 1912 to Theodore Curtis Fugate and Minnie Florence Fugate in East Prairie, Missouri, the second of seven children. She joined a sister, Virginia Inez, who was fourteen months older than she. Thelma gained another brother, Curtis Christopher, when she was about two years of age and she was later joined by Wiltz Theodore, Grace Elizabeth, Billy Taylor, and Clayton Andrew.

Thelma was born with a caring heart, and from a very early time took on the role of a second Mom. She was always concerned and quite serious about things, but at the same time, a playful little girl that liked to climb trees and play rough. She described herself as a "tomboy". Her older sister, Inez, was a very frail child that suffered from asthma and wasn't able to play or do much. Mom told about how they shared a bed when they were young, and how, at times, she wouldn't get much sleep due to the wheezing going on beside her. She also remembers Papa walking Inez up and down on the outside porch, just trying to help her breathe, and Mama rocking her hard to do the same. Thelma's sensitivity resulted in concern and worry in many situations. Inez eventually outgrew the asthma to some extent when the family moved to a drier climate and possibly outgrew some of the problem as she reached adolescence.

My mother, Thelma, described her parents as loving dreamers that one might term "hippies" in today's terms. Theodore was a fur and hides trader and traveled a lot. Mom told of times she would welcome her "Papa" home and love to hear stories he would tell. Her "Mama" was very creative as she would make up games and plays with the children and read and tell stories to them about how obstinate and spoiled she was as the youngest child in her blended family. Having a piano because of her great love for music, Mama would often play for them and they really enjoyed the music.

They didn't have much music elsewhere like radio etc. yet. At times they would go to a theater and view vaudeville, stage entertainment with song and dance, and watch black and white movies with no sound other than a piano to add drama and excitement. The family and friends would often go nut gathering in the Fall which was always a fun thing to do, and the children would gather the different kinds of nuts, and later take them out of the shells to enjoy just eating them or baking things with them. Papa also loved to fish and hunt, so the family moved quite often because Papa was looking for a "better fishing spot".

One frantic time Mom told me about was when her brother, Curtis (Bo, as he was called) got lost in the woods when he was about six years old. Papa had all the people from their small town helping him search for about fourteen hours, when all of a sudden a far-away neighbor came bringing Bo up on a white horse. Mom was SO worried, and SO happy to see him.

The Fugate family must have had many adventures with seven children. Their material wealth was not great, but their love and times together instilled in all of them a deep love of family, and they remained close-knit and good friends throughout their adult lives. Mama made the most of Christmases even though there was very little money. She would do what decorating she could and bake special treats for them. Not having a Christmas tree every year, they would hang their stockings on a chair or on their beds and receive nuts, oranges and maybe dried fruit the next morning. Mom told the story of receiving a box in the mail one day close to Christmas. As she moved it and heard a sound, she thought it was a baby raccoon. She was so worried about it she begged and begged her Mama to open the box. Mama just smiled and said they would have to wait until Christmas. How Mom worried about that and the fate of that 'raccoon'. Mama knew what it was, but Mom didn't. Mama had ordered a "mama doll" for Thelma for Christmas and once the wonderful day arrived, Thelma got her surprise, one of the first talking dolls.

In moving quite often the Fugates at one time lived on a houseboat, which seems so unlikely for a family with small children. At one moment Thelma ran to her mother and was crying desperately that she had "dropped the baby in the water!" As Wiltz was a baby at the time Mama began seeking the help of all around when after about ten minutes noticed a baby doll bobbing in the water. What a relief for Mama and Papa.

As was mentioned earlier, Thelma seemed to take on much responsibility in the family. With Inez having health problems, Thelma took on the mother's chores at times her mother was ill. She washed many diapers and cooked many meals before the age of ten. During times when they were quarantined for various illnesses, Thelma was the one who carried out the necessary chores. She did, however, suffer herself from Typhoid Fever when she was young.

Thelma talked a lot about her aunts, uncles and cousins. These were also Fugates. Her one maternal aunt was her only other aunt. Her Father's brothers and sisters and their children afforded Mom some fun visits during her childhood, and also some time to compare temperaments as her one uncle was pretty gruff and not much fun. She told the story of spending Christmas Eve with a cousin and giggling and talking late into the night. Pretty soon she heard her aunt say, "Santa, I guess you will have to skip our house because the girls aren't asleep yet." Then, coming from the girls' bedroom, "We're asleep, Aunt Dorie, we're asleep".

Thelma loved taking trips with her Papa which she often did. "Young Thea", a name she was given by friends in town, felt pretty special going on these trips. Papa would also take her to the barber shop to get her hair cut and on occasions her ear clipped. She envied her sister Inez's beautiful long curls, but for some reason she was given the "Buster Brown" hairstyle with the bangs. I guess they felt that suited her best. One time on one of their trips to town there was a town hall meeting in which they were giving away a car. As wide-eyed Thelma was taken with all the festivities, standing close to the stage, she was asked to select a ticket for the drawing. The winner of the new Ford was so elated he gave this little girl five dollars. She was so happy she gave one dollar to Inez and one dollar to Curt and she also bought herself a red rain cape and some matching rubbers to go over her shoes for three dollars. That was such a big surprise occasion for her.

It was during one of these trips with her Papa that Little Thea witnessed something that would stay with her for a long time. There were some colored people standing in a group singing a song and meandering around. Mom asked her Papa who they were, to an answer that he gave of, "Those are poor folks that do not have very much, and I don't want you ever thinking you are better than they are". I'm sure as time went by, Mom understood what her Papa was trying to tell her.

Thelma always loved school even though she had to sometimes walk pretty far to get to school. There were no school buses for her at that time. I guess she was quite social from an early age, as she told the story of having to sit in the wastebasket at school as punishment for talking too much when she was in first grade. She was pleased to win a district spelling bee in the eighth grade and often talked about being the Fairy Godmother in an operetta in which she also sang a leading song. It was about this same time that she was one day jumping off her porch to the yard, when at one point she fell on her back and sustained quite an injury. Not able to talk immediately, when she caught her breath she pleaded with her Mama not to take her to the doctor, that she was alright, when truth has it that it was at that time that she had fractured a bone in her back. It hurt her for a long time, her activities were very limited, and ex-rays taken when she was an adult showed a bone in her back had been broken at some point in her life. As Thelma matured, her high school days were filled with lots of work, with chemistry being a favorite subject. She dreamed of someday becoming a pharmacist.

As life involves lots of adventures and experiences, one of those offered to Thelma was a trip to California to help her Aunt Pearl, her maternal aunt, in a restaurant in Lomita. She finished high school there at Narbonne High School and worked for her aunt in the restaurant. It was here in the restaurant where she first met Ishmon Gaw, who worked in the oil fields and had come to California from Tennessee at the suggestion of his brother who also lived in California at that time. Evidently Ishmon had many meals at the restaurant and did enough talking to Mom, that he discovered he really liked this little gal. He also dated Mom but Aunt Pearl was very protective and would only approve her dates if she could also go along. So that is how Mom got to know my future dad.

Missing her family, Thelma went back home to Missouri to visit and figure out what to do next. When she walked in her house she noticed a beautiful baby boy on the bed in the bedroom. It just so happened to be her new baby brother, Clayton Andrew, eighteen years her junior, about which her Mama had kept a secret during correspondence to California. At first Thelma thought it was her sister, Inez's, baby, since she had married quite young. Inez did have a baby but this one wasn't hers. Mom had difficulty leaving home again with Clayton, her baby brother, at home. There was not much opportunity, however, in East Prairie for Mom, so she left and went to Greenville, Mississippi to seek work and found a job in a bakery. Making many donuts, and other goodies she met some nice people and gained some more confidence. After working for the bakery for awhile, she then went to Louisiana, to help open up a new bakery. It was during this time that she met some young men and began dating. She had a good friend, Lola Mae Stevens, with whom she had many good times including double-dating. She became engaged to Cade Britt, who, according to her was a great dancer, and a great person, likening his looks to that of Bing Crosby. She began to question her love for him because after her engagement she became infatuated with a couple of others, and in the long run, she couldn't vision herself as a farmer's wife, since farming was Cade's love. There were others that peaked her interest, and she was also continuing to write to Ishmon. As she often said "I was very fickle".

The Fugate children back: Curtis, Wiltz, Bill, Clay,
front: Inez, Thelma, Grace

It seems that Ishmon Gaw, who was smitten with her from the start, issued her a proposal, in a letter, to come and join him in California. Although it was difficult for her to leave her family behind, she knew the opportunities in East Prairie were so limited, so she ventured to California. Ishmon had sent her some money for a bus ticket and met her when she arrived. The move for her was an adventure and love she couldn't ignore. Ishmon was the youngest of eleven children and had left the rest of his family in Tennessee, so here they were, Ishmon, being fourteen years older than Thelma, starting their life together.

Thelma and Ishmon

Teddy and Thelma

Keck and Teddy

When Thelma Fugate came west to marry Ishmon Gaw in September of 1934, Ishmon, who had the nickname, Keck, was working in the Kettleman Hills of Kings County in the oil fields, and not in Lomita where the two had met. They were married in the court house in Hanford on September 17th, and attended by a jeweler who had sold Dad Mom's wedding ring. They then moved into Dad's little house in Murray, a community made up mainly of oil field workers. After being given a "chivaree", a form of hazing in which they were put in an enclosed trailer and pulled all over the countryside, not knowing where they were, they were given a shower by their neighbors and they started their marriage in a crazy way in Murray. Thelma made the most of things by making gingham curtains and a skirted dressing table to give the place a "homey" look.

Their neighbors, Gordon and Evelyn Sangster, became good friends and helped them a lot when their first child, Theodore Curtis, was born on February 15th, 1936. Being quite a distance from the hospital, Evelyn, an experienced mom, helped by taking Thelma to the Dr. on occasion and helped after Teddy's birth. This wide-eyed little boy was a joy and was named after his grandfather.

Thelma, becoming a little homesick and wanting to show off her new little guy, made a train trip to Missouri to visit family when Teddy was about six months old. During this trip Teddy became very ill and Mom had to return early. He had severe diarrhea and was becoming dehydrated, due to the possible change in water and formula. Mom went through a trying period in which she had to feed him very carefully and slowly until he recovered. It was quite worrisome but he gained back his strength in time.

Mom and Dad had an opportunity to move into one of the bigger houses in Murray and that gave them a little more space and more enjoyment. It was at this time that they met Joe and Eleanor Peters, who also became good and longtime friends. Mom was pregnant again and Eleanor gave Mom a baby shower. A second child, Nancy Ann, was born to Thelma and Keck on April 22, 1938. Thelma didn't let her parents know that she was expecting until Nancy arrived. I guess it was a "get back" time for when her baby brother, Clay, was born. Nancy was about thee weeks earlier than expected, and weighed a little over five pounds. It took about three days to name her. Keck liked Bonnie for a name, but Mom kept thinking of the dog in the neighborhood that she kept hearing being called, "Here, Bonnie, Here, Bonnie". Mom thought of Sarah, which was actually Keck's mother's name. The nuns at the hospital discouraged them by mentioning, "She's much too pretty. She'll just be called Sally. They eventually decided on Nancy Ann, a name Mom had heard over the radio before Teddy was born, and one she had always liked.

When Nancy was about four months old they moved to Lemoore, leasing a farm with two cows, three pigs and one hundred chickens. Not having the experience doing this sort of thing, I suppose they thought it was a challenging adventure. Thelma often had to deal with the animals by herself, as Keck worked different shifts and sometimes was gone at night. The story of pigs escaping their pen one afternoon was one Thelma had to deal with trusting that Teddy would hold onto Nancy's baby buggy while she ran after the pigs. That he did and all was well, until the chickens escaped now and then. She also had to gather eggs, and clean and grade them to sell.

Keck and Thelma had the opportunity to buy their own place, also in Lemoore, on Champion Street, about one mile from town, and made the move when Teddy was about two and a half and Nancy was about nine months. They had sold the cows and pigs but kept the 100 chickens, and decided to add some rabbits to the inventory. They worked hard and made it a great home they would live in until Keck retired. It was here where they became the neighbors of the Harrahs. The Harrahs had seven children, the youngest two being comparable ages to Teddy and Nancy. Their other children were, Juanita, Jack, Bob, Billy, and Barbara. Dean and Lorraine became almost everyday playmates. Dean, the first few times of visiting, would bully Teddy by pushing him off his tricycle. After about three times of observing this, Mom told Teddy to fight him the next time he did it. Teddy did that very thing, and it was the last time the pushing was done. When Nancy was about two, she jumped off the porch step and knocked out one of her upper front teeth. Unfortunately she had to do without the tooth until her new one grew in when she was about seven. She was given the nickname, Snag, by her Uncle Wiltz.

Nancy and Lorraine became like little sisters and the best of friends, playing dolls, making mud-pies, eating sour grass, and doing many things together, including joining in on family vacations. Nancy was afraid to go into Lorraine's house sometimes because Mrs. Harrah loved parakeets and would often let them fly around, which Nancy didn't like.

Thelma made another trip by train to visit relatives in Missouri when Teddy was four and Nancy was two. It was a brave move for Mom to venture out on a three day, two night trip on a train with two little ones, but Mom did it. She said we were so well-behaved, but I know she prepared us well with talk and toys as she received many complements from the porters. She told the story of another lady, with children about the same ages as we, who was traveling also and how those little ones ran up and down the aisles, swinging through the seats, and dirtying up the dining cars, as their mother ignored them and sat reading a book the whole time. The porters only rolled their eyes at them. I don't remember the train trip. I do remember, however, sitting in my grandfather's lap at a dinner table. I don't remember how he looked, as I was more entranced with the glasses on the table filled with something red, perhaps Kool-aid. I also remember my cousin, Earl, Inez's son, pulling me in a wagon and passing by an old building with people singing. In retrospect, it was probably a church. I also remember the wagon turning over but I survived. That was the last time we saw my grandfather. He later died of pneumonia and problems with Diabetes in a hospital and was laid to rest on the day of the bombing of Pearl Harbor.

Childhood of Teddy and Nancy

Mom always regretted not being able to go back for my grandfather's funeral. At the time my grandfather died my Uncle Wiltz was in the Coast Guard, and as World War two progressed, my other uncles joined different branches of the armed services, Curt, in the army, Billy, in the Air Force. Clay, when he became old enough, joined the Navy and then the Air Force.

When I was about three and Ted was in Kindergarten, we were in a parade in downtown Lemoore on Halloween. The school kids always dressed in costume and paraded down through the town and ended up back at the school and watched Halloween movies and had treats. We didn't know what trick-or-treat time was. Mom had made me a red-riding hood costume and Ted was Superman, and we held hands and got to lead the parade down main street.

When I was in the first grade I was playing on the bars at school, and fell and sprained my arm. It was very painful and the first of many falls. I had to wear a splint on my arm for a long time, and it finally healed up.

Grandma and Clay came to Lemoore to visit us when Clay was twelve years old and in the seventh grade. Clay went to school for a short time in Lemoore. I think he got a few smiles and comments because he "talked different" coming from a Midwestern state.

During the war Aunt Pearl had moved to Benicia, California, with her husband, who had been in the Navy, and they lived in a little house by the bay. Inez and her husband, Collie, had also come to the Bay Area and were employed in the shipyards in Vallejo. There was an arsenal that was hiring in Benicia, and Aunt Pearl suggested that Grandma come to Benicia and apply at the arsenal for work, and that she did. Florence had never held a job outside of the home. But she was positive and at fifty-two impressed her employers. She was hired, and moved up to supervisor and felt proud of herself to do all this. She bought a new little house that became a wonderful gathering place when all the aunts and uncles and cousins got together. I used to look forward to our visits. I loved all my uncles and aunts. They all had such a wonderful sense of humor. They would entertain us beyond belief, and keep us laughing. My Aunt Inez should have been in movies. She was like a Lucille Ball, a real comedian, without meaning to be. And all of my uncles had their individual style of humor, and they were fun. I loved to play with my cousins, Sharon and Alan, Lynn and Mark, Ronnie, Dennis, and Gary, all enough younger than me that I felt I could mother them. I remember taking my little cousin, Sharon, who was about two and a half at the time, to see the Wizard of Oz. I marveled at how she sat still for the whole movie, really engrossed in all the action. Now, other than Earl, Inez's youngest son, I am the oldest of the remaining cousins.

Mom and Ted and I made several train trips from Hanford to Benicia to see Grandma and relatives living there at different times. I always loved riding on the train and remember the scary feeling I experienced going from one car to another as I watched the moving parts below us. Sometimes when Dad drove us to Benicia, we got to cross the bay on the ferry from Martinez to Benicia if we made it by a specific time, as the ferries only ran at certain times. If we didn't make those times we had to travel around a longer way. Being so prone to car sickness, I ways hoped to catch the ferry. As I got older I would often spend a couple of weeks in the summer with Grandma. It was always fun. Grandma didn't drive or have a car so we walked places or took a cab. She would order groceries and have a cab pick them up and deliver them. She loved to go to movies. So while I was visiting we would go about three times a week to see a movie. She taught me how to cook a few things and it was a wonderfully memorable time for me. We made a few trips to San Francisco to attend the Ice Follies, which was a great treat. I always wished that Grandma could be that little white haired lady that was presented a bouquet of roses at each show. Grandma loved the horse races at the fair each year, and could be quite an excited spectator when watching, as was also the case when she attended the roller derby games. Grandma was such a pleasant, fun person that melded well with all her children and grandchildren. She was the only grandparent I had and she was very special.

Nancy and her cousins, behind, Dennis, Alan, Ronnie,
Sitting: Gary, Sharon, Lynn and Mark

My Grandma

Thelma became involved in the local Baptist Church and Sunday School as did Teddy and I. Lorraine and her sister Barbara often went with us. It was here where Teddy and I decided to become a Christian, and were baptized by Reverend Fletcher. The church played a big part in our lives as we were growing up. We did, however, change membership to the Presbyterian Church when I was in high school. I think Mom felt the Baptist Church was a little too conservative for raising teenagers who needed to have a little fun once in a while.

Thelma was gifted with many talents. She made most of Nancy's school clothes from kindergarten through high school. As Nancy grew older there were many fun trips prior to the pending school year to see the styles of the ready-made dresses for that year. Then off to the fabric store to plan and buy fabric for specific styles. She was a genius for creating anything. She made Halloween costumes. She often made matching outfits for Lorraine and Nancy. She once made a whole wardrobe for Mary, a little friend, the pastor's daughter, who had lost her mother. She helped her plan and made about ten dresses as she went off to college. She made Lorraine's wedding dress when she married Wilton Wyman, one of our neighbors, and a good friend of Ted's. It was a beautiful white faille suit. With matching pillbox hat it was the perfect thing. She also made a majorette uniform for Nancy's friend, Roberta, out of purple and gold corduroy, our school colors. Roberta accompanied us when I marched in the high school band. The last treasure Mom made was a christening dress for her great-granddaughter, Hannah. It was beautiful and Mom loved working on it. I feel I learned so much about sewing from Mom and still love working and creating with fabrics.

Thelma was not afraid to try anything. She often told the story of feeling badly about not taking Nancy to school on her first day of kindergarten, because she had taken the job of mail carrier, and had to fulfill that duty. A neighbor, Mrs. Lowe, who had three boys, was delighted to take a little girl to school and Nancy wasn't upset by it at all. Ted and Nancy walked to school since the house was about a mile away. It was not within a bus district. One of the mail carriers, Mr. Taylor, who lived in town, was one that Mom substituted for. I remember being at his house, sitting in a booth in the kitchen, and learning my right hand from my left hand. To this day, I can vision him telling me that my left hand was the one inside the booth closest to the window, and I can still remember that moment, and how I learned right from left.

Dad had to drive about thirty miles each way to work each day. The San Joaquin Valley can be very foggy in the winter time, and miserable to drive in. One time we traveled the same road my dad traveled to go visit my aunt and uncle who lived in Avenal at the time. On the way back which was early evening, we had to creep along in this thick, thick fog. It was awful. I can remember my mom saying how bad it was that my dad and others had to drive this road every day, and it didn't even have a line down the middle to help. So the next day she wrote a letter to the road commissioner to tell him about this problem. It wasn't a month later before they had a yellow line down that road. Hurray for Mom! It was also on this road that we were traveling along one time during the day that I had opened Mom's purse, as kids sometimes do. The window was open and out flew my dad's paycheck. We turned around and searched for a long time to find this piece of paper, among the plowed fields. We did find it, but it took awhile.

We also had other neighbors, besides the Harrahs. When I was about seven, the Smiths, Harold and Jenny, with their two girls, Betty and Naomi, built a house between us and the Harrahs. They were a very nice family, and we enjoyed visiting with them. The Parkers, on the other side of the Harrahs, were a family with eleven children. I remember Mom rescuing Mrs. Parker one time by taking her to the hospital after one of the children had drank some kerosene. It seemed like something was always happening in the neighborhood.

Mom had an interest and talent for photography. At one time when Teddy was about nine and Nancy about seven, she and her brother, Clay, started a photograph studio in Lemoore. Both of them loved photography and Clay had gained the experience of working in a studio in Benicia. They were kept quite busy with developing film, to photographing individual portraits, to some weddings and more funerals than you might think. I remember walking from school with my friend, Roberta, up town to the studio and hanging out trying to stay busy, since I couldn't go home and stay by myself. The business lasted for about a year and a half when Clay decided he wanted to go back to school, and Mom decided she needed to be home more, so they closed it down. Dad built Mom a little developing studio in the back of the house, so she continued to work at that a little longer, mainly developing film.

Ishmon worked his difficult shifts, one week on days, one week on afternoons, and one on graveyard(midnight to morning), in succession. Then, with four days off, he would start all over again. I don't know how he was able to adjust to it, but he never complained and never missed a day of work. There were some times in which I would accompany him to work and see the big compressor plant with all the big noisy machines.

Amazingly, he could instantly tell by the sound if one quit working or was having problems. I can remember sitting under a big water cooler having lunch with him on these days feeling quite special. At times we would spot some scorpion spiders in the surrounding area. Dad liked to putter in his work shop with little engineering feats and was good at fixing things. With barely a fourth grade education, he was a self-taught man that I admired. He loved music and detective stories. I still love to look at his banjo that he would sometimes take out and strum.

He loved to garden, raising tomatoes, onions, squash, potatoes, beans and even asparagus. He loved to cure olives, and he loved to experiment with grafting trees to get new varieties. I remember standing out with him as he irrigated the rows of vegetables one by one. It was during this time I came eye to eye with tomato worms that so closely match the leaves they are on. We always had more vegetables than we could eat, so Ted and I, at times, would position a little stand down by the road under some large palm trees and try to sell our produce. It wasn't too profitable. Within those palm trees lived some owls that we often heard that added a little excitement. There were times that we would have three kinds of tomatoes on the dinner table: green fried, sliced beefsteak, and stewed. At times when I balked about eating certain vegetables, My dad would say, "You have to learn to like them", which I did eventually do. Mom would spend many hot days of summer canning foods and making jams and jellies. One of the favorite treats we had were pomegranate trees. Ted and I loved them and couldn't wait to sink our teeth into those juicy seeds. Mom dreaded us eating them because of the stains on our clothing following our indulgences.

Mom did most of the disciplining. Dad had a sort of commanding look and he didn't have to say much in order for us to get the message. I can only remember Dad spanking me one time, and I deserved it. He always listened to the news on the radio at a certain time of day. I was crawling around his chair at this special time one day making noise. He asked me to be still and quiet, but I continued to do my thing. He reached over and gave me a spank with his hand. I feel, though, it hurt him more than it did me. Mom did most of whatever spanking had to be done. I can remember her telling us we could not go over to the Harrahs at times, whereas we would sneak over there anyway. I can remember her coming after us with a ping pong paddle, as we came running with our hands behind our backs. I also remember her calling us back home with her two-syllable and two-pitched names, Nan-cee, and Ted-ee.

I did love school and remember having many friends. When I was in first grade I would get upset and complain to Mom that Jerry scribbled in his coloring book or a boy pushed someone off the bars. I liked all my teachers and enjoyed reading and spelling, especially, winning a fourth-grade spelling bee with the work, GEOGRAPHY. I felt pretty special when I received a lot of valentines on that fun day. I did well through elementary school with the exception of book reports, which I detested.

The Christmas Season was a fun time for us to anticipate and experience. We would usually be in a pageant of some kind at the church and our little town of Lemoore would decorate store windows and do the usual festive things. We had a long, narrow living room with linoleum on the floor which did lend itself to roller skating one Christmas when we received skates from Santa. I can remember Mom trying to keep us quiet that Christmas Day as my dad slept. It seems that he always worked the night shift on Christmas Eve and therefore had to sleep on Christmas Day. I remember Ted and I crawling in bed with Mom early Christmas mornings and having to wait until Dad got home to go celebrate the tree and all its beautiful surroundings.

I remember seeing Santa Claus one Christmas Eve. I was ill that year, and Mom set up my bed to be in the living room with the tree. I remember seeing Santa pass by our long narrow window in front of the tree. I remembered that for a long, long time and continued to believe because I HAD SEEN HIM! Mom used to talk about how hard it was to fill the stockings with all the noisy bells on them.

One year we had a wedding on Christmas Eve by the tree. It was really beautiful with candle holders in the background etc. My Uncle Wiltz married my Aunt Betty that year. He looked so handsome in his dark suit, and she was beautiful in her white satin gown. It was a great year because we had a house full of relatives that had a lot of fun together. I also remember it was that year that Betty and her twin sister, Helen, had made me a life size cloth doll that they had to hold all the way down on their lap in the car. It was a really neat doll! I loved dolls of any kind and Ted loved airplanes. He made many models and hung them from his bedroom ceiling.

We were given the experience of having two wonderful dogs during our childhood. Tommy, a little white mixed breed, during our early years, was a friendly companion that had experienced somehow a broken tail, so could not wag it, but he smiled when he was happy. Our other dog, Dizzy, part cocker and part dachshund, would go fetch the paper for Dad and lay by our toys if we left them down by the road. I remember Mom's bravery when she had to rescue his little body after he became blind and deaf, but still stayed by our toys and was hit by a car.

Ted and I had a great back yard to play in, complete with large cottonwood trees, one in which we built a tree house and from which hung a tire swing. Although there wasn't much of a lawn, I remember many days digging and making roadways with a hoe to play toy cars with my brother. I remember Teddy teasing me by chasing me around the property with a fist full of nothing, but me thinking all along that he had bugs or spiders of which I was petrified. I remember wanting to dress like my big brother with jeans and sailor hats, and playing soldiers together with our helmets and toy guns. I also remember the time we were on rationing using food stamps, and a few air raids with blackouts when certain planes flew over. I remember Mom taking her lookout duty at the local tower down the road from our house.

Mr. Harrah, Dean and Lorraine's father, sometimes would rescue us in the evening if there was a problem and Dad was working a night shift. There was one time when Mom wasn't feeling well and was resting. Ted was at a neighbor's playing and I decided to go play on the tire swing. When I walked toward the swing I encountered a huge gopher snake, at least three feet long, and quite big around stretched out right under that tire swing. I gasped and ran into the house to tell Mom. "There is a big, big, big, big snake under the swing", with my eyes getting bigger with each word according to Mom. We called Mr. Harrah and he came over to take care of the problem. Although gopher snakes are not dangerous, they have a frightening look to them and are very prevalent in the San Joaquin Valley, as are rattlesnakes. Another experience I had with a gopher snake left a lasting impression. Mom and Dad raised rabbits and chickens. The rabbit hutches and chicken coops were a little way from the house with a path and garden vegetables in between. One evening when feeding the baby rabbits, we found one missing. Not far from the hutch was another large gopher snake with a big lump in the middle. My dad chopped the snake open with a shovel and in amazement my eyes fell on this little baby rabbit, still whole, but dead, and it reinforced the whole idea of how snakes use their prey. I learned much about the life and death of chickens as we often would have chicken and rabbit for Sunday dinners. I witnessed chickens being prepared for food from the chopping block to remove their heads, and the plucking of feathers, to the dinner plate on the table. I remember the problem solving of which Mom was so good. One of the good egg producing hens was found to have an enlarged chest and crop and wasn't eating. Mom felt she could fix the problem, and as I watched Dad hold the chicken, Mom doused the crop with alcohol, slit it open, cleaned out all the green stuff inside and sewed it back up again with a needle and thread. I was so awestruck over all of this. The hen lived quite a lengthy life following the operation and continued to be a good egg producer.

As Ted and I grew, we enjoyed playing Kick the Can at dusk with the neighbor kids and baseball at the golf course across the street from our house. We earned a little spending money at the Harrahs during the summer. They had an apricot orchard, and we would pick and pit apricots and place them on trays to dry. Our profits we would spend maybe swimming at the local pool or maybe going to see a movie. We enjoyed our bikes and also roller skating when the yearly portable rink came to town in the summer. I enjoyed being in a Girl-Scout group and we did a lot of activities from day camps to decorating graves with flags on Memorial Day and Veterans Day, selling cookies, having swim parties, ice skating in Fresno, and having lots of fun.

When Ted was in the seventh grade he had quite a mishap. During the daily physical education time he and some friends, Dean Harrah, being one, were playing football. When he was running for the ball, the boy in front of him ducked instead of blocking and another boy ran into Ted, hitting his two front teeth. As a result, he had to have those teeth pulled and replaced with false teeth. The one thing that upset him the most was the worry of possibly not being able to continue playing the trumpet which he enjoyed. He did, however, continue to play. Ted had artistic talent and loved drawing things, especially charicatures, and later in life tried oil painting and seascapes. The ones I have are very special to me.

In Junior High School I joined the orchestra and played the percussion instruments, bells(xylophone), triangle, kettle drums, and had a short stint with a cello, but didn't care much for that. I remember thinking my seventh grade teacher had a grudge against those of us in the orchestra because we had to leave class to participate in the music program. I think she was trying to impress on us that we still had to keep up with our school work even though we wanted to be in the orchestra. Looking back it was at that age that children begin to resent things a little more when told to do something. As I got older, I realized this about Junior High students. I also joined a little majorette group in seventh grade and we marched and twirled our batons in our green satin skirts, and white tops and boots. Mom and Dad bought a piano and I learned to play it and enjoyed it a lot but never became very proficient on it. I continued to enjoy it as I was growing up, and dabbled in playing some favorites when I wanted to express myself. I felt so fortunate to have it in my life. I continued the bells when I entered high school and became a member of the band. It was a favorite subject for me partly because of our great teacher, Mr. Weiss, and the friendships I made, going to football games and marching in parades. I became closer friends with Nancy, who played the clarinet, and Roberta, who was a majorette. One embarrassing moment happened during a parade that remains with me. As I was pounding along on the bells, the ball on the end of my mallet fell off and rolled away down the street. I couldn't just stop and pick it up because it rolled out of sight. So I just kept playing with the stick as if nothing was wrong. Pretty soon Mr. Weiss, our teacher comes walking up to me and brought the ball. I was so relieved and he gave his usual little smirk that was his trademark. We had lots of fun times together, including playing with Roberta on the High School Tennis Team. I was given the nickname of either Twinkle-toes, or Slew-foot depending on the outcome of the game by our coach, Miss Schendel.

Jr. High baton group

Graduation from High school with
friends Sue (left) and Evelyn

Band uniform (purple&gold)

I don't remember feeling pressured to "have what all the others have", as I feel some youth have today. Brand names that stood out in my world at the time were: Levi, Buster Brown saddle shoes, cashmere sweaters, Pendleton pleated skirts and shirts, and Lanz dresses. In our community of mainly middle class, we all accepted each other for whom we were and enjoyed each other. We were thrilled to receive a new pair of Levis or a new pair of shoes but didn't feel we had to have a particular brand. When I was in high school girls didn't wear pants. They had not become popular yet. We wore dresses, many times with full skirts, and pleated wool skirts and sweaters, with scarves around the neck. Saddle oxfords were the thing and rolled down bobby sox completed the look. I grew up with Doris Day, Rock Hudson, John Wayne, and Alan Ladd,

Lemoore is a rural town with outlying farms and dairies. Many of my friends were Portuguese, hard-working, loving people. Because of my associations with them and my coloring, I have often been thought to be Portuguese. I am actually English, French, and Irish on the Fugate side, and Scottish and English on the Gaw side.

I knew my dad's ancestors had come from Scotland, and that has always held interest for me. When I was about fourteen my dad's cousin, Verdie Gaw, came to visit us. He was married to a cute little lady from Scotland, Margaret. After their visit with us, Margaret wanted us to visit them in San Pedro, California. So Mom and I took a bus down to visit them. It was a long trip with loads of traffic in the Los Angeles area. As we watched out the windows of the bus, we felt we really got to know the travelers in the cars next to us as we slowed down and sped up our pace on the busy freeway during commute time. It was fun to meet Margaret's sister, Nessie, and her son who dressed in his kilt and whole Scottish regalia for us. He had been in several movies when they needed Scotsmen. I was quite impressed. They took us to lunch at a very nice Hollywood restaurant. To a fourteen year old this was a fun time, as I watched for any movie stars that might happen along. I did see Ricky Nelson, a popular singer at that time, leaving the record company parking lot in his snazzy blue convertible. The other thing I remember about the trip was Nessie serving us lemon meringue pie, which I really didn't like. I could not refuse it, however, and managed to get it down. I guess it was another one of those things I learned to like.

When I was in high school, we didn't have the alcohol and drug problems that are so rampant in today's society. Perhaps I was naïve in thinking it just wasn't done, and maybe some did use alcohol, but I wasn't aware of it, and my friends certainly weren't either. I suppose the most daring thing we did was go to the drive-in movie theater with one or two in the trunk to save money. Of course, later we all enjoyed the movie together.

Decorating the gymnasium for a dance, especially a formal dance, was a very exciting opportunity. By the time it was completed, it didn't resemble a gym. It felt rather special and added to the pride we had in our school. The tickets were reasonable and many could afford to attend. The extra expense for a dance might be a dinner beforehand often at the Chinese restaurant in Hanford, or indulging in something sweet at the Superior Dairy. I wish the simplicity of all we had was more popular today.

When you were a senior at Lemoore High School there was a special day all seniors looked forward to. It was called "Senior Sneak Day". On that day the seniors planned a get-away trip for the day and didn't have to attend school. I remember we went to Avila Beach for the day. There were about eight of us girls that spent a great day together. As we frolicked on the beach in our swimsuits and wide-brimmed hats we climbed on some rocks, tried making pyramids with our bodies and just had so much fun. What added to the pleasure were some boys from Cal Poly Tech School in San Luis Obispo that just happened to be there also. A lot of flirting took place and it all made for some interesting conversation on the bus trip home. Unfortunately, we were all so sunburned the next day that wearing a low neck dress was not even comfortable.

I remember attending my first funeral when I was about fourteen. One of the girls I knew was killed at the County Fair on a tilt-a-whirl ride. It was a very emotional time for me. The next funeral I attended after that, which was for a distant relative I really didn't even know, was equally difficult. I just had such a time dealing with the sadness that is felt in such a situation. I have, of course, in time, been to many funerals, which are difficult, but are a part of life and a time for closure when a life ends.

It was also about Junior High School age that I had a couple of "fainting" spells, that led to tests for thyroid problems etc. but really never led to anything conclusive. I suppose it was just the age. We did a lot of folk dancing in Junior High, which I loved. Mom had made me a great skirt, at least I thought it was. It was a three-tiered red skirt with white ball fringe between the layers. I wore white pantaloons under it and a white peasant blouse with it. It was pretty cute. One day we went to see a parade celebrating centennial time, so I thought it might be fun to wear this outfit. Well, about half way through the parade I got quite hot and passed out. When I came to, I thought, "It's a good thing I wore my pantaloons." It kept things a little more discreet.

Another time that I felt one of these spells was when we were visiting a friend in the hospital who had a broken arm from falling off a donkey while playing donkey basketball. As we walked into his room, I saw him laying there with his arm at a right angle with a pin through his elbow. For some reason, this all really got to me and again I passed out. I experienced this feeling a couple of other times when we encountered accidents etc. I guess this was one reason I never felt I could be a nurse.

My friend Lorraine

Lorraine and Nancy vacationing in Redwoods

Every summer my dad would take a two-three week vacation and we went camping. Sometimes we would go to the mountains and sometimes to the beach. Reflecting back this wasn't much of a vacation for Mom because she still had to do the household chores with more dirt to contend with and fewer utensils to cook with. However, in discussing it later in life with her she enjoyed the diversion and doing something in a different environment. Dad was a creature of habit, finding that if he liked a place, why not go back to that same place year after year, and that is about what we did. After experiencing the valley heat in the summer it was always a treat to catch some of the coastal breezes in Santa Cruz. We would load up our car to the point that Ted and I would be sitting on blankets, boxes etc., and space was at a premium. I would always pack crackers to munch on to keep car sickness away. I also found that trying to sleep was a good thing to do. A couple of years we had to take our little dog, Dizzy, with us so we had some difficulty finding a pet allowable campground. So the one we had to use did have a great donut shop nearby where Dad, each morning, would supply us with the delicious treats.

Then we discovered a campground right outside the city limits of Santa Cruz along highway nine, called Sycamore Grove Resort. With large wooded sites, a river and beach close by, hiking trails, big night-time campfire, dance floor with a juke box with even some folk dances and the latest hits, such as Nat King Cole, Rosemary Clooney, Patti Page, and many others, ping pong tables, shuffleboard courts, big tire swings, and a small grocery store, it was the perfect place. We felt secluded up in the mountains and yet a five mile drive would take us to the beach and boardwalk, a perfect place for any age. We would often take a friend and sometimes we would meet up with acquaintances from the previous years. Lorraine Harrah went with us and she and I really had some good times there. This is where I learned about Snipe hunting. One summer as we got together with some of the other younger people who were vacationing there, one of the older boys asked if we would like to go to the hobo camp. Not knowing what he was talking about, we said sure. There were about eight or nine of us, and we walked through the woods and through a culvert, that had a little water in it. All of a sudden we came out in a clearing, and we saw some little huts that were put together with sheets of tin and a little of everything. Sitting beside one of these little houses was a little old man dressed in tattered black and wearing a hat. He was very friendly. The railroad ran pretty close by to the houses which consisted of about four, and we found out that the railroad men would sometimes throw things out to them. They had their own little community, and even though it had a lot of junk, they had it pretty well organized. There were even little flowers planed around the area. It left a lasting impression with me. I guess all of my early days there instilled a big love of the area so much that I would eventually make my home there in those mountains.

About the time Mom needed another job she began praying about one. She received a call from Mr. Engvall, the elementary school principal, asking her if she would be interested in driving the school bus for the elementary school. Not being something she even considered, she wondered why Mr. Engvall would even think about asking her. She thought about it, was excited, and knew she could do it. This meant having to obtain some special licenses, but she passed all the tests with flying colors. From that position she went to driving for the high school. She said the voices were better to listen to than the shrill voices of the little ones.

Mom, as the rest of her family, had a great sense of humor. I can remember how we would celebrate April Fool's Day. There was one time she wrapped up a bunch of broken glass and items, and put them all in a big box and wrapped it up for mailing. She put it down by the roadside and watched to see what happened. There were a few people who would slow down and look at it, and drive on, but at one point a man slowed down, passed it up, backed up and picked it up, and drove up our driveway. Mom couldn't keep a straight face, and she and I hid in the bathroom, and didn't answer the door. He left it at our door anyway. Another time one of her brothers tied some string around a new tire, and left it in the road. As someone started to take it, he pulled the string and it jumped. The person knew he had been had.

Mom had a lot of sayings that were quite funny, and she knew when to use them. It seems that people coming from the Midwestern part of the United States use these sayings more than most people. Perhaps those from other parts have their own. These sayings always added a colorful and entertaining picture to the situation. When I began teaching, and often read children books with some of these sayings in them, I often had to explain them to the children. I hope these colorful expressions are never lost. It is such a wonderful part of our heritage.

When I was in high school, I worked at the local theater, as did Lorraine and my friend, Roberta. We ushered people in, kept order with any loud, noisy children, cleaned up sunflower seed hulls after the movies, and you might say babysat children that would come in on Saturday at three o'clock when we opened and stay until nine o'clock when their parents would return. It was only twelve cents a child so it was a pretty good deal. Adult seats were forty cents each and the loges (rocking chairs) were fifty cents. Unlike today's theaters, you could watch the movies as long as you like, and not have to clear out after the showing. There was always a double feature, and short news reels too. The most difficult thing we had to endure was the cigar-smoking men that would come out to the lobby for their vice and the smell it left in our clothes. Mr. Leino, our boss and theater manager, was a nice, friendly man who would ALWAYS bring us maple bars for a snack. Never would he deviate from that-it was always the same—MAPLE BARS. To this day I can not stand to even smell one.

Since I often worked on Friday and Saturday nights, I was tied up until at least nine or nine-thirty. So when we had scheduled dances at the high school, we would often have to arrive late, after we finished our shift. Lorraine and I would sometimes end up double dating and having a sleep over later to talk, giggle, and relive the events of the evening. What great memories!

When Ted was a senior in high school I was a freshman, so I got to know a few of the "upper classmen", and developed some 'crushes' on a few of the guys. One of his friends, I felt, was very funny and I decided to invite him to a backwards dance in which the girls ask the guys to go. I thought it would be a real fun night, but I remember feeling very disappointed as he just clammed up and wasn't as funny as I was anticipating him to be. He was much more fun when he was with a group. I went along with my dad to practice driving with Ted before getting his license. As we wandered off the road onto the shoulder and field, my dad calmly told him "You have to use the rear view mirror, but ALSO look ahead of you to see where you are going". I'm sure Ted would have preferred me not being along.

When Ted started college at Fresno State, and I was a sophomore I dated a young man I had met at church. I was impressed by him and his beautiful voice when he would often sing solos. We dated for about nine months but I tired of him and we broke it off. I did get to attend a fraternity dance with him in Fresno. I really felt special and wore a beautiful formal gown that Mom made for me. It was coral chiffon and she worked so hard on it, making fabric rosebuds with rhinestones for dewdrops, making it just right. I still have that dress. As for the young man, Lorraine began to date him. She eventually tired of him too. He was a nice guy, but not for us.

Ted hadn't really decided on his field of study at college and at that point wasn't really goal oriented. He knew he didn't want to stay home and chop weeds and wasn't sure what he wanted to do. He did love aircraft and at one time did some help loading for crop dusters and worked in mosquito abatement, both unhealthy jobs, but these certainly weren't life time goals. He also carried mail for awhile, but he tired of that. So one day he went and signed up for the Air Force. Mom and Dad weren't real thrilled, and this was another opportunity for Mom to worry about the outcome. However, they finally respected his decision and he was off to Lackland Air Force Base in Texas for basic training. From there he was assigned into the intelligence division and transferred to Monterey, California to study the Russian language. We did get to see him on occasional weekends and there were times he would bring a friend home for the weekend, so that was fun. One weekend he brought two friends home and Ted and his girlfriend, Lorraine and one of the guys, and I and the other fellow all went to a formal dance. We all dated together in Ted's red and white convertible, sitting on laps in formals. We had such a wonderful time, laughing and dancing away. My date was from Mobile, Alabama, with a super thick accent, and was hilarious. That was one of those times that Lorraine and I spent the rest of the night just talking about the fun we had. Ted's final destination while in the Air Force was Trabzon, Turkey where he lived in a house with about ten other men, working near the Russian border. He set me up to correspond with a young Turkish girl that was one of their neighbors. That was delightful. I still have some tatted doilies she sent me.

During the time Ted was in Turkey I experienced a spiritual moment that I still think about today. Before Ted had joined the Air Force he had dated a nice little gal from Hanford, Diane Wright. Diane had been to the house for dinner a few times, and the one that Ted took to the dance that I mentioned earlier. We had met her parents once, if I recall, but weren't close friends with them on a regular basis. One Sunday morning as Mom and I were preparing to go to church, I just happened to mention to Mom my dream I had just had, "Mom, I dreamed Mr. Wright, Diane's father, died last night". "Really, that's strange!" We hadn't heard of him being ill or anything. Nothing more was said about it. Then on Monday morning Mom read something in the newspaper. "Nancy, you're not going to believe this, but Mr. Wright passed away Saturday night". I didn't know what to think. We later found out that Diane had been with her father, holding his hand that night when he died. My deduction is that perhaps she was thinking of Ted so far away and somehow I absorbed those feelings. I've often had strong feelings about things, to find that I was right on. My mom and I have always experienced thoughts and feelings of similarity often to saying the same thing at the same time. There is so much we do not know about the human spirit, but hopefully some day will find out about.

When I was a sophomore in high school, Mom, my grandma, and I took a bus trip to Illinois to see my Aunts, Inez, and Grace and their families. Inez was married to Howard, a quiet, nice man and, having two sons, Jack and Earl, at an early age, was now helping to raise her grandchildren. My aunt Grace was married to Art who was always up for a new game of cards. We got the chance to see some new country when Grace and Art took us up to the Wisconsin Dells. It was beautiful, with some swimming and pick-nicking with all the cousins. I can remember pick-nicking with them and sitting down at the outdoor table until our side of the table filled up faster than the other. Can you guess what happened? Over we went with all the food flying through the air and landing on us, a time of laughs never forgotten.

The Greyhound Bus lines, even though an express, seemed to take a long time, three days and two nights, to reach our destination. We were so tired of sitting that we all wanted to lay on the bus floor and put our feet in the seats. When we stopped we had to decide if we wanted to use the restroom, or get something to eat, never enough time to do both. It was a fun but tiring experience.

About two years later Grandma, Mom and I made the trip to Illinois again, this time in a Ford Falcon my parents had bought for me. I loved my little black car and we made some wonderful memories on that trip. It became quite hot at some areas and with no air conditioning as we stopped for refreshment I remember Grandma say," I don't know whether to pour this in me or on me". At one time Mom was doing the driving and I was sitting in the back seat when all of a sudden the car had gone out of control and started to tip. There had been a thunder storm earlier which had left some water on the road that caused the sliding of the car. Grandma popped up with, "Thelma, where are you going?" to which Mom responded, "Well, Mom, I don't know!" It was a scary moment, but Mom righted the car and we were on our way. On that trip I met some relatives for the first time in Missouri and got to see lots of pretty country. On the way home one of my favorite cousins, Ronnie, Grace's son, came with us. He was about six years younger than me. He had a wonderful sense of humor and kept us entertained as we came back through the Grand Canyon, listening to his favorite rock and roll music on the radio, slathering me with QT, a sun-tan lotion, and stretching his neck to see the big trees coming down through California. Ronnie was always a lot of fun when we got together, and he will always be a big part of my special memories. Unfortunately, he passed away way too soon, and I still really miss him.

Mom obtained a job at the local Crocker Anglo Bank in Lemoore and I continued on in high school enjoying every bit of it and still today it leaves me with wonderful memories. I had so many good times with my friends Evelyn, Sue, Nancy, Roberta, Anna, and so many others. I really enjoyed my senior year, and dated a boy named Tommy. He was a brother to Stan, my friend, Roberta's boyfriend, and eventual husband. He was a real sweet guy that was very handsome and could at times be an Elvis look-alike. I remember him giving me a little blue radio for graduation which I thought was wonderful. We had a great graduation and I surprisingly received a citizenship award that evening. It was supposed to be a surprise for our whole family, but my Mom happened to be in a jewelry store picking up a ring for my eighteenth birthday in April, and the lady let it slip that "She must be very proud of her daughter". It seems they were engraving my name on a plaque for the school. It was a very special surprise for us. Our class reunions have been wonderful and afforded me time to see those friends again. There was one reunion that George and I had planned to attend at Harris Ranch, which is about thirty-five miles from Lemoore on Highway five. It was a multi-class reunion spanning about four years. George, due to his work, at the last minute, was unable to make it, so I asked Mom if she would like to go with me, and she did. It was fun, as many alumnae remembered her and were so happy to see her. Some rode her bus and others just knew her because of the lady she was. Our high school was and still is the most beautiful school I have seen. The pride of Lemoore High School lives on as it has expanded but kept the Spanish architecture with its beautiful tiles and arches.

While I was in high school I taught Sunday school, enjoyed it, and it was at that time I thought I would like to be a teacher. So after I graduated, I did have some goals in place. We were very fortunate in Lemoore to be able to take a free bus from the high school to attend the College of Sequoias, a junior college, in Visalia, about twenty-five miles away. It was here where I would take my lower division courses and still live at home. It worked out well. Then I would transfer to Fresno State College to complete my work and obtain my degree.

As I was working on my second year at College of Sequoias, Ted had finished his stint in the Air Force and had returned home. He looked great, was sporting a beard, looked thinner, and seemed more settled. I remember his comment about Mom. "She's so much grayer than when I left". I'm sure she was. If worrying develops those gray ones she earned every one.

After graduating from College of the Sequoias I transferred to Fresno State. Sue Beck and I decided to share an apartment with two other girls in order to stay in Fresno and not drive it daily. It was also a learning experience for us. The other two girls and Sue and I first rented an apartment over a garage close to the Fresno State campus. Most of our classes were at the new campus being built on Shaw Avenue, but bus service from old to new campus was available. One of our roommates was from North Dakota and about three years older than us and was working on getting her California teaching credential. She shared her room with a gal Sue had met through her brother. She was also a little older and divorced. She was returning to school for an education in something. Two of us would be in charge of housekeeping one week while the other two shopped and cooked meals, and then we changed duties the following week. Unfortunately, the divorced gal didn't hold up her end of the bargain. She partied all night and slept all day. The girl from North Dakota returned home the following year and I believe married within a year. Sue and I obtained a new apartment with two other roommates for our senior year and did much better as we finished working for our degree.

Ted decided he wanted to study Psychology so that is where he put his efforts. On returning to Fresno State he took the required courses, and obtained his degree. It was also during his years at Fresno State where he met his future bride, my sister-in-law to be, Bonnie Nicole Ellis. They married, Ted continuing his studies while also working with the Juvenile probation department in Fresno. I continued my classes and student teaching and was ready to move on. I feel so grateful to my parents for allowing me the opportunity to continue my education. Neither of them was able to receive this precious gift they had given me. To both of them education was extremely important and their sacrifices were, I feel, many, but Insignificant to the rewards they felt.

As we were engrossed in college, Mom and Dad decided to do a little remodeling on our house. I can remember how hard both of them worked. It was laborious work, and Mom wielded that hammer just about as well as Dad. It involved putting in a new ceiling and roof on one part to enlarge the living room area, and I witnessed a bruise on Mom's hip and buttocks, that was horrible. She had fallen through one part of the ceiling. She was alright, however, other than being sore for awhile. She said when it was all over, that she enjoyed the work and challenge it had been, and had a good feeling of accomplishment.

Ted at 20

A lasting portrait of Ted

It was now time for me to experience a little of my own independence as I began to seek a teaching position. We had recruiters come from the Bay Area to hire teachers for a fast growing area in Hayward. We were also given some other leads to help us find employment. Of course, my dad wondered why I just couldn't go to the Lemoore School District and work there. Then he would have me close to home. Mom seemed to understand why I wanted to go elsewhere, although she hated to see me break that bond, too.

My friend, Sue, with whom I went to high school and roomed with in college also wanted to venture out. She had come from a family of eleven children and had worked very hard baby-sitting all through high school and doing what work she could to put herself through school. Her father, a contractor, didn't see the need for a girl to seek further education. So Sue and I put out feelers and eventually both got accepted in the Mount Eden School District in Hayward, a wonderful jumping off point for a new teacher. We got an apartment to share and got off to a great beginning.

As I was beginning my career, Ted was beginning his family and welcomed a wonderful baby boy, David Curtis, into his life. Mom's and Dad's first grandchild brought so much joy into their lives and continued to do so as he grew. He was such a cute little gentleman, curious about everything, and like a sponge absorbing everything in his surroundings.

As Sue and I taught in Hayward, we at first had a drive of about twelve miles from where we had our first apartment. Sue feared the fog which we had to deal with in the winter, so we decided to move closer to our jobs into a different complex. We knew of the complex because some friends we knew from Fresno State, Angie and Patty, lived there. They were also teachers, but we all taught in different schools. The principal at my school had a reputation for being difficult and demanding. I trembled with nervousness each time he entered my classroom and stood in back of the room with a smirk on his face. It all taught me to be well-prepared as our plans were scrutinized each week, a great preparation tactic. I survived him and worked for many other principals in the future who would not have given me that great first start. It was exciting having my own classroom, preparing bulletin boards and meeting new students each year. My first year I taught at the Ruth Gansberger School, and was then transferred to Mohrland School to teach the following year while the Argonaut School was being built. I was slated to teach there. When it was finished the next year I felt so privileged to teach in a brand new school. It was a kindergarten through fifth grade school built in the round with a central courtyard. Sue taught in a different school in the district, so we would share stories at the end of the day.

During the time Sue and I lived together, I decided to venture out and do something different to my hair. I envied Sue, who was a dull-blonde, kinky-haired gal in high school. She now had her hair straightened, bleached, and wore it in a French twist which was very attractive on her. One Friday evening after work I decided to have my hair colored and I picked out a nice auburn swatch that I thought would be nice. During the process of having first to apply bleach to lighten my dark hair for the color, I was shocked that it hurt so much. I thought to myself, "Sue goes through this all the time?" Then when the color job was finished I was shocked how red it was. It was almost orange. I looked like one of the monkeys with red hair and dark eyes and brows. I couldn't tell the beautician I hated it. I just left. Sue had gone on a date and wasn't home. I just felt so weird. I hadn't planned on going home to Lemoore that weekend, about a four hour drive, but I made a quick decision to do so at eight o'clock in the evening. On the way home I heard truck drivers honking at me and I don't think it had to do with my driving. My new look must have been quite bold. When I got home, which was late, my parents were already in bed and weren't expecting me home. I tied a scarf around my head before retiring into my old bedroom. I knew Dad would not like what he saw. He always hated even things like nail polish, calling those who wore bright things as such "painted ladies". The next morning Mom came in my room and was just glad to see me. I really felt disappointed in myself, however, both my parents were so great. Neither of them said anything derogatory. I think they sensed my regret. Mom happened to have a hair appointment on that Saturday. And she let me take it. However, when the beautician took one look at my scalp she would not touch it. I had blisters on my scalp, and they did not want to take any chances of a law suit if they inflicted further damage. Well, Mom suggested we go to the drugstore, get the darkest brown shade of haircolor we could find and she would carefully apply it to the strands with a toothbrush. That she did and it calmed it down a little. I drove back home on Sunday. When I went back to work on Monday morning, I had early morning yard duty. All my little charges came running up to me with, "Miss Gaw, what did you do to your hair?" All I could think was, "You should have seen me before this". So that was my big color changing experiment.

Sue and I were also experiencing city life and going to some places unlike we had in Lemoore. Being adults we would sometimes go to a bar on weekends. We, as beginning teachers, were kept pretty busy during the week. We tried a few different kinds of cocktails when we ventured out. My Uncle Clay went with us at one time to San Francisco. I drove in my Ford Falcon and remember the steep hills especially on California Street. My uncle introduced us to vodka gimlets which I thought were much tastier than martinis. My very first drink had been on my twenty-first birthday which in today's world is hard to imagine. My boyfriend at the time asked what I would like. Not knowing what to get I ordered a martini. I thought it was terrible and couldn't understand how some people like them.

So, one day later on Sue and I were driving from Hayward over to Benicia to visit my grandmother. At the time my Uncle Clay was there with her. To show how naïve I was about alcohol, I decided to stop at a bowling alley bar on the way thinking, "I'll take my uncle a vodka gimlet", knowing he liked them. So into the bar I walked in innocently asking, "May I please have a vodka gimlet to go?" The man looked at me quite strangely, and said, "To go where, Maam?" I stupidly said, "Well, I wanted one to take to my uncle." He then laughed a little and said, "Lady, if I gave you a drink to go, I would have the ABC all over me." Yes, I had to ask what the ABC was. So my lesson was learned. You don't get drinks to go. When I told my uncle about the incident, I don't think he believed me, or didn't dream I would not know the impossibility of such a deed.

Sue and I also got to see our first opera, Aida, in San Francisco, as we were experiencing city life. The upscale shops, theaters, and restaurants were quite a contrast to what we grew up with, and it was a great experience to be able to enjoy some of it.

After working so many years in the compressor plant for Superior Oil in the Kettleman Hills, my Dad decided it was time to retire. Mom's and Dad's love for the coast took them to Santa Cruz for their new home. They bought a wonderful older home in an established neighborhood that had lots of charm about it. Mom wasn't quite ready to retire and ended up finding a job for a short period of time at the Ford Mercury dealership in Santa Cruz. The office manager at that time was a very difficult woman to deal with as Mom used to tell me, and must have truly been because Mom could get along with everyone. So that job came to a close but she obtained a job for the county of Santa Cruz in the treasurer's department. It was a wonderful job for Mom. She loved the people and they loved her. She made many longtime friends there as well. She worked another fifteen years there until her retirement. She became famous for her gift of writing poetry about and for all occasions and people with whom she worked.

While all this was happening in Santa Cruz with my parents, I was having some exciting times in Hayward. My friends and I would often, especially on weekends, go out to dinner, and one night we stopped at a piano bar afterwards for a drink. The waitress came up to us while we were there and announced that "Mr. Darr would like to buy us a drink, and would like to know what we would like?" I thought, "Who? I don't know anyone named Mr. Darr". I was quite cautious about accepting a drink from someone I didn't know. About that time this nice-looking gentleman came over and introduced himself as George Darr. I remembered seeing him occasionally at the apartment complex in which we lived, and obviously he had seen us. So I did feel better about the whole offer. He was there with some others from General Motors after completing a class, and one of the nurses in the class urged him to come over and get acquainted. Well, as things progressed we ended up all going to a place that had dancing. That is how I met my future husband. We continued to become friends, and continued dating. He was divorced and had two sons, about nine and eleven at that time. I was hesitant about getting too involved due to a relationship I had experienced in college in which I dated a man for awhile only to find out later that he was married with about two or three children. He had been a real deceiver, and hurt my pride quite heavily when I discovered the truth.

George showed me his divorce papers, and I felt much better about pursuing our relationship. One of our first dates was down to meet his sister, Inger, and her family, in San Jose, and the rest is history. We had the boys on weekends, and we would sometimes take them to dinner and or movies. He sometimes cooked dinner for me. He even helped me correct papers from school. He was a wonderful gentleman and great companion.

On one of our dates we had gone to a party with some friends that worked with George. As people do at cocktail parties, they were meandering in and out of the kitchen. As George and I walked into the kitchen I heard one of the men ranting and making jokes about negroes. He seemed obsessed with this subject and I had heard enough. I hadn't said too much up until then, and I surprised everyone by saying, "Well, I'm one-fourth black." I've never seen anyone try to backtrack so fast in my life. He didn't quite know what to do. I never said anything else about it. I guess they all asked George later if I really was part black. I do hate prejudice!

Working at General Motors George had purchased a new little Chevrolet Corvair. It was a beautiful cherry red and he had supervised the paintjob himself and it was a beauty. The day he picked it up he came and got me and we went to his friend's house. It happened to snow that day, while we were there. I hadn't experienced falling snow before and I guess I appeared to be more excited with the snow than the great little car.

We went to San Francisco to see Glenn Yarbrough and the Limelighters sing at the Purple Onion, a well known nightclub. Other musical groups we enjoyed were the Serendipity Singers, Harry Belafonte, Dean Martin, and so many others.

George and I dated for about two years before marrying in Santa Cruz at the Presbyterian Church not far from where Mom and Dad lived. Like a true gentleman George asked my father if he would give his permission to marry me. I remember listening from the kitchen and hearing my dad say, "Well, if that is what you want to do". Mom wasn't too happy with my decision at first. Perhaps it was the age difference of about nine years, or the fact that he was divorced and the father of two children, but she did eventually accept it. I was so excited. I couldn't wait to start my life with him.

On November 18th, 1962, at 2:00 in the afternoon we "tied the knot". George still teases me about the fact that I called him many times that morning at his motel, to "make sure I was going to show up". I don't know why I called, just last minute nerves, I guess, and I was checking on things that were to be done. Mom and Dad gave us a nice reception at the house with about fifty people. Again, Mom showed her love and talent by making my wedding dress. At the time we married I had switched roommates. Sue had married and moved. Angie, one of the friends at the complex and I had become friends and what a friend she was. Her previous roommate had gone to Europe for awhile, so she and I got together. When we were planning our wedding, which was going to be over Thanksgiving vacation, I knew I wanted her to be a bridesmaid. I had saved the maid of honor role for Lorraine, my longtime friend and closest thing to a sister. Angie had been in a wedding recently and had worn a beautiful rose-colored satin dress. I loved it. Again I went to Mom to get her thoughts. Off to the fabric store we went. We found some rose-colored satin that looked like the same fabric of Angie's dress. Mom made another dress for Lorraine that looked identical to Angie's. This all set the design for my dress, the same design but long sleeved and in white embroidered satin. Mom had painstakingly sewn many covered buttons down the back. It was all beautiful. I keep my dress in my cedar chest with the rose formal Mom made me for the fraternity dance.

Ted, who was still living in Fresno, came to the wedding but Bonnie couldn't come because she was expecting their second little one and the doctor didn't want her traveling. So Ted left her at home according to him, "playing Buddha". George and I went to Monterey that night and had a fabulous dinner in Monterey down by the water, and spent the evening at Casa Munras, a nice hotel in Monterey. We went to Carmel the next day and down Highway One to the Los Angeles and Hollywood area in that pretty little red Corvair. I was not feeling well the day after the wedding. I accused George with of pouring me too much champagne, and it didn't sit too well. We toured Hollywood and that area, had some nice dinners out and just took time to enjoy one another. It was the first time I had celebrated Thanksgiving with just two people. But we had a wonderful week and returned to Santa Cruz to open some great presents we were given. When I returned to work the following week my class and I had to get used to using the name "Mrs. Darr" rather than "Miss Gaw".

Angie had moved in with some teacher friends in Alameda, but ended up moving back to Fresno at the end of the school year, to help out her parents, a wonderful little Italian couple whom we often visited, Vito and Connie. We use to refer to their house being the "best restaurant in Fresno". They fed you from the time you arrived until the minute you left. I can still picture Connie standing at her stove and stirring her spaghetti sauce. Vito was a little man filled with energy and creativity. When they all came to see the model home after we decided to live in Pleasanton, Vito climbed under the model to make sure all was built to his specifications. After that he made a wood carving of the house. Angie was such a special person in our lives and lives in our hearts as we remember her hospitality and fun spirit she offered. She was an outstanding teacher and touched so many lives in such a beautiful way. I was very blessed to be her friend. We lost her shortly after we moved close enough to enjoy her. She was a one-of-a-kind. We both miss her very much. She left a great sister, Louise, and brother-in-law, Augusto, who are the proud parents of Ivan and his wife, Alyssa, and their two grandchildren, Nickolas, and Marina, who are about the ages of our youngest grands, Gabe and Grace.

My beautiful little niece, Kimberly Ann, was born about a month after George and I were married, so another joy came into all our lives. I will always remember her birthday, as we were married on November eighteenth and she was born on December thirteenth.

Our wedding day

My wonderful attendants and friends Lorraine and Angie

Connie & Vito and me in front of our model home

During our first year of marriage George and I moved into a triplex in San Lorenzo. Our landlord was a nice middle-aged bachelor that lived with his mother in the back unit. He was quite an artist and did wonderful water color works. Another nice couple, Gary and Ann lived in another unit. They became parents about the time we did and we enjoyed some fun times with them. They moved back to Pennsylvania to be close to family and we lost touch with them after awhile. The hardest part of our marriage was the fact that George worked nights at the Fisher Body Plant in Oakland, and I of course, taught during the day time so we didn't have much time other than weekends to see each other. We wrote notes to each other a lot. We did manage to start picking out furniture for our abode. Our first piece of furniture was a redwood burl coffee table that George had made. We had picked up the piece in the Santa Cruz Mountains and he had worked on it at the first apartment we lived in after we were married. It was beautiful, with a free form with nooks and crannies in it. He also made a very nice record cabinet out of mahogany. He had several records when we married, and he often teased me that I married him only for the record collection. I told him he married me to get rid of my Ford Falcon, with him being a General Motors Man. We bought a very nice stereo with a mahogany cabinet and enjoyed listening to great music on the weekends. It was exciting deciding what kind of furniture to get to start our life together. We seemed to love the same style and colors so it was easy deciding. We obviously didn't buy just for the apartment, keeping in mind we would eventually have the furniture fit a house. So we opted for a large white couch, a turquoise club chair, a gold rocker, a big brown lounge chair and a beautiful Karastan rug with jade and dark gold and brown in it. It looked great with the burl coffee table and the record player and cabinet. We also bought a nice bedroom set, considered to be Italian Provincial, which we loved. A small dinette set finished things off.

I got to know the boys, George and Gregory even better. On one Easter vacation we rented a trailer and decided to take a trip up to northern California and Oregon. Going up through Eureka and camping in the redwoods with the boys was a lot of fun. We motored on to Shasta Lake, Crater Lake, and the Oregon Caves. We saw lots of damage the recent flood at that time had done when the Rogue River had overflowed, and saw many houses turned upside down. We had lots of snow near Crater Lake and had some rain on our adventure. The warmth of the trailer and the hot chocolate moments were much appreciated. We made a trip to Disneyland and Knott's Berry Farm with them and had a great time. The boys would often tease me in some way, by putting fake spiders on me or telling me little fibs about themselves. George and Greg, being very different from each other, sometimes got into a few little scraps, expected at that age, but they had some good moments together too. When we took the boys to dinner we could always depend on Greg ordering chicken, and George trying something different. George would always have a book, and Greg, a bat in hand. They still are very different in their interests, but I guess that is what makes up our world.

Greg and George

Enjoying a gift from Gregory

Greg and Debbie Darr with 1st great-granddaughter,
McKenzie standing-Jamie, Scott, Aubrey, Eric

Son and daughter-in-law George and Crystal Darr

Near our first anniversary George came home one morning with bleeding stomach ulcers. He had had a busy, stressful night at work, and all of it hit him hard. He had had this problem once before so he knew what to do. He asked me to call his doctor and he got into bed. I went to school very early that morning and made sure my lesson plans and work papers were all in order and called for a substitute. On calling the school I found out that the brother of one of my little students had hung himself the night before. When I got back home I took George to the hospital and got him settled. Then I went back home to get some pajamas and a robe to take to him. As I was driving back to the hospital I heard on the radio the news that President Kennedy had been shot. I thought that day would never end. George had to have several pints of blood, and was in the hospital about a week and a half. When he saw Jack Ruby shoot Oswald he thought he was watching a Television movie. What a week that was! He healed up after spending Thanksgiving in the hospital. He insisted I spend the holiday with my parents so that is what I did.

Within a couple of years George was going to be transferred to a new General Motors plant opening up in Fremont, and we were looking to get into a house, so we began looking at houses all the way from San Jose,

Saratoga, Fremont, to Pleasanton. We looked at many, many tracts. We were now getting down to reality just what we needed and just what we could afford, seeing that location had so much to do with the prices. One week-end, on the way back from visiting Angie in Fresno, we came by some models we had looked at already in Pleasanton. We decided to take another look. There was one model that seemed to be the perfect fit for us, so we bought our first house, an exciting time. Our furniture we had purchased when we lived in the triplex looked beautiful in our new home and in time we completed the other rooms.

George did a wonderful job with the yards, doing some brick work and building a retaining wall in the back yard which was a lot of work. We met some wonderful neighbors and life was good.

George and Greg were getting older, and one of the first parties we had in our house was a surprise birthday party Greg gave for his girlfriend, Debbie Thomas, who was to later become our daughter-in-law. Both boys were getting through their teen-age years, and were busy doing school things. We often didn't get to see them quite as much as their activities were much greater. George, being fourteen months older graduated first and started some college courses and was dating Crystal Souza, who also graduated the same year. They decided to marry on January First when they had both turned eighteen. Unfortunately, we were not able to make the last minute decision occasion, but George's mother was with them. They seemed so young but seemed to know what they wanted. Living in an apartment at George's Mom's, they continued some school and eventually went to work for Dalton Booksellers. They worked up to managers and eventually were transferred back to Minneapolis, which was a great experience for them.

When Ted's two little ones were about two and four, he and Bonnie decided to move to San Carlos south of San Francisco to start a new job. He worked there for the Juvenile Dept. working with Juvenile Delinquents, testing etc. After a couple of years there he took a position in Martinez, California (Bay Area), again working for the county in the Juvenile division, and they bought a house in Pleasant Hill. This is where David started school. From there they moved to Antioch near the water and

Ted got the idea of life on the water. When David was about eleven and Kim, nine, Ted and Bonnie made a major decision about their lives. Ted was a little disheartened and burned out about working with so many juveniles with so many problems. He felt the need to spend more time with his own children and got the idea to purchase a sailboat and to do some traveling. After living on board the boat for about fourteen months to acclimate themselves, they decided to "take off". They secured a course of study from a correspondence school for the children and "set sail". Sailing from San Francisco to Santa Cruz and then down the coastline, to Mexico, Through the Panama Canal, San Blas Islands and Columbia, they spent two and a half years of this life style. Kim and David became very experienced sailors and developed a wonderful sense of accomplishment and learned a lot about the sea and our southern neighbors. They even got to go aboard a Jacques Cousteau boat and became quite self-reliant. After experiencing piracy around Columbia, they set sail for the United States. Seeing the Florida coastline on Easter Sunday, they put foot on land and decided to make Pensacola their home. Bonnie was so good about corresponding during this voyage, but there were some times that went by where there was no news. It was another worrisome time for Mom and Dad. Dad, not wanting to alarm Mom, contacted the Coast Guard and they were able to get in contact with The Grand Turk(name of the ship). When they came for their first visit after their trip they were tan, slim, in great health and glad to be back.

Mom and Dad had moved from the big home on Van Ness in Santa Cruz to a four-plex they bought on the east side of Santa Cruz. All was not well, and they decided to separate. This was a rough time for me emotionally. I knew during my younger years there had been some problems, but they always seemed to work themselves out. I knew that their interests differed. Mom was a much more social being than Dad and had to do things alone if she wanted to go places. Dad was happy with simple things. Mom liked having nice things. Communications between them were poor, so it was expected but hard to realize. Mom had moved into an older Victorian apartment at first. Grandma had retired from her job at the arsenal, and had come to stay with Mom. Mom then bought a house close to West Cliff Drive which she had for awhile. It was while she was living here that she had a heart attack, thought to be her gall bladder, and was in the hospital for a couple of days. As I recall, she lived in this house for a couple of years before she sold it. Dad seemed lost without Mom and I felt quite torn as I visited them.

I taught for two more years when we moved to Pleasanton teaching First Grade at Alisal School. About September before my last year we began paperwork to adopt a baby. George had the two boys and although we weren't picky we requested a baby girl. He had played ball and did the things with the boys but wasn't sure he would be able to do the same as he knew he would be older when they needed him for those things. So we worked with the Children's Home Society in Oakland for about nine months getting paper work, references, money etc. all in order. We were told the timing is unsure. It could take anytime between six to twelve months before you have a baby, so we waited. I had committed to that teaching year. In the meantime we did ready a room for a nursery, painting it pink with a pink rug, and purchasing a bassinet. That summer the day school was finished I said, "O.K. I'm ready. Where's my baby?" Chance would have it that our baby girl was born on the Thursday that my year ended on Friday. But they waited the usual three weeks to introduce her to us. We received a call to tell us they had a baby girl for us and asked when we could come in to see her. We hadn't shared our adoption plans with anyone except two immediate neighbors that we wanted to use for references. Adoption can sometimes be difficult and changeable so we were pretty tight-lipped about it. The next morning George called into work to take some time off for personal reasons. I got up early and laundered some new diapers and baby gowns I had put away. I fixed up the bassinet. I had made a fancy little skirt for it. Then that morning off we excitedly went. When we arrived at the agency they took us to a private room and brought the baby into us. She was a sweetheart as she squirmed in our arms. They left us alone for awhile with her and then came back and asked us what we thought?

I had met a lady in our neighborhood who had adopted from the same agency. She had told me about their procedures. She said they call you in to view the baby. Then they let you go home and discuss it to make sure you want the child, and you go back the next day to pick the baby up. Well, when the social worker asked what we thought, we were both taken with this little doll. Then she said, "Would you like to take her with you?" We were so excited to think we could take her home that day. We both said, "Of course!" How could we say no? So she came home with us in her little gown and blanket they supplied. When George and I got around the corner we pulled the car over and both cried in happiness. She became Laurie Ellen as she joined our family.

George went back to work that day and passed out cigars much to everyone's surprise. We had a couple of shocked people in the neighborhood also. I couldn't wait to take her down to Santa Cruz and show her off to

Grandma and Grandpa. Our little dog, Zipper, who had been "King Pin" all along was quite curious, but turned out to be a wonderful, loving and patient companion. Motherhood brought some changes to my life although I loved most of them. Our neighbor, Evelyn Boyer, threw a baby shower for Laurie and she got to attend. She was a little fussy that evening, and everyone wanted to try and soothe her. I discovered later that she was a little too stimulated by many people around her and felt better soothing herself in a quieter environment. Her adoption became final about one year later in court. As we waited for our turn with the judge, Laurie, in a little white bonnet and dress, crawled like a little crab to avoid dirtying her dress. We felt a finality with that day and settled in to watch her grow.

When Laurie was about eight months old, Greg, the youngest son, had graduated and decided to marry his high school sweetheart, Debbie Thomas. It was a beautiful little wedding in a Hayward Lutheran Church. After they married, they took their Volkswagon van and traveled across country to see new territory all the way to Pennsylvania to see some of Debbie's relatives. After being gone for some time they returned to Hayward, helping with finances along the way by picking cherries, an example of their hard work to acquire what they have wanted in life. After settling down, they presented us with a grandchild, Scott Gregory. Later moving to Oregon where they thought opportunities would be better and where Greg and George's mother lived, they produced two more grandchildren, Aubrey Lynnell, and Erick Lee. They purchased forty plus acres in the beautiful countryside of Falls City, out of Dallas, Oregon, and worked hard to give their children a look at life with animals as Four-H became a big part of their life. The grandchildren now all have children, totaling eight great-grandchildren for us. Scott Married Jamie, and they have McKenzie and Hunter. Aubrey and Chris are raising three little girls, Serenity, Madeline, and Kyra. Eric and Melissa have Braden, Caitland, and Annika. They are all quite involved in sports and all are beautiful children. We certainly wish they were closer. They have sent photos and updates on their activities and accomplishments of their family. Greg and Debbie also now have a nice little beach house about fifty miles from their home in Nescowin, Oregon, which is delightful and about two blocks from a large beach and the ocean. Unfortunately our trips north to Oregon were limited as our girls were growing as were the demand of work.

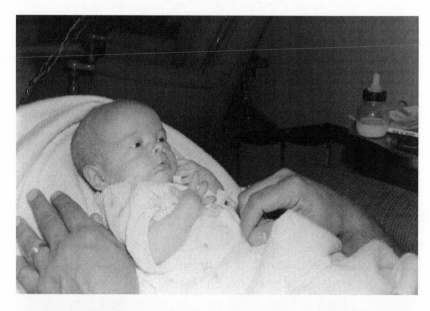

Our first baby girl, Laurie in her daddy's lap

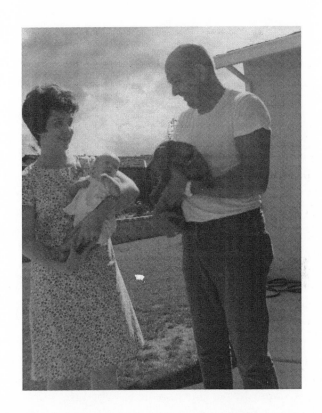

Our 2 children, Laurie and Zipper

Our wonderful Zipper

George and Cris also moved to Oregon after their time in Minneapolis. George decided to go back to school and pursue an engineering degree. Finishing his education at Oregon State in Corvallis, Oregon, he was hired by Bonneville Power in Portland and eventually became in charge of the Alternative Energy division, especially well-versed in the wind-power division and windmill construction, and did some traveling to Wyoming and other places to develop this type of energy. Cris continued to work in the book industry and also found employment for a veterinarian and was able to enjoy animals she so loves. They also bought forty plus acres in a beautiful spot, out of Willamina, Oregon, and have developed it into a wonderful home filled with their accomplishments. George is a perfectionist woodworker, creating much of their own Oak Mission Style furniture. Their home is a showplace with Cris's beautiful quilts and cushions and artwork depicting their travels to such places as Greece, Egypt, Africa, Central America, and soon to be Galapagos islands and the Amazon region. They have helped us out in so many occasions.

When Laurie was about twenty months old we decided to adopt another little girl, so we applied again at Children's Home Society in Oakland. This time we had another little bit of sunshine about eight months later. Again when we went to see this new little baby girl, we were taken with her. She seemed to have a little smile on her face (at three weeks), was very blond and fair, unlike Laurie, who was more olive skinned with dark eyebrows, but blue eyes. This new little girl looked a lot like George's sister's children, especially like her younger son, Bobby. So she fit right in with the family. In fact, later on at times when Inger, George's sister, would sometimes babysit for us, her friends and acquaintances thought she was one of the Robinsons. We named our new little girl, Luanne Elizabeth, and she joined her big sister, Laurie, who was also taken with her. The names Laurie Ellen and Luanne Elizabeth were names George and I agreed to, and decided upon because we liked them. I later realized that my dad had two sisters, one named Ellen, and one named Elizabeth. That wasn't my reason for the names but it just seems to be one of those little coincidences.

As the girls grew along with Zipper, we had a lot of fun times. I wanted to be home with the girls, but decided to earn a little cash by baby sitting other children also when they got older. So I took care of some for maybe two to three hours, and a few on a daily basis. It worked out well, except sometimes at lunch I would have ten to twelve for a short period while their mothers played tennis or shopped. I sometimes would sit them on the floor in the kitchen in a big circle and give them peanut butter sandwiches and milk. I don't recall any problems except the whines sometimes when the parents picked them up. It was after one of these pick-ups that we experienced a great tragedy. Our little Zipper had gone out the front door when a parent came to the door. Unfortunately, he continued across a semi-busy street and was hit and killed by the car. That was very difficult for all of us.

My dear friend, Lorraine, was experiencing some problems with Wilton, her husband, about this time. I mention this because of how dear she has always been to me and a big part of my life even though we haven't lived very close to each other once we were grown. Wilton and Lorraine had two wonderful children, Jim and Leslie, when they divorced, who were about nine and eleven. As life gives us some strange and often bewildering experiences, Lorraine was later introduced by a friend to a very nice man, David, who had lost his first wife to an automobile accident. Well, the rest became history as they dated and married. Lorraine then had four more children to blend with hers, ranging from nine to eighteen. The amazing thing was David's two girls, Theresa and Lavonne, and Lorraine's daughter, Leslie, all had reddish colored hair as did Jim, Lorraine's son. David's two boys, Dale and Rick, had Lorraine's dark hair, blue eyes and freckles like Lorraine. It was a marriage made in heaven. David was the son of missionaries and was born in Africa where he had lived until he was sixteen, a heritage he embraced and one he eventually shared with Lorraine as they took a trip to Africa together. When we visited them in the foothills of Fresno, we were amazed at the dynamics of the group, and the groceries they would purchase on their bi-weekly shopping excursions. I'm sure there were rough times for them as they reared all those teens, but because of their strong faith and Lorraine's great spirit, they endured everything. There are now many grandchildren and even great-grandchildren in Lorraine's life, and it is always a delight to visit them. David passed away in 2006, from a strain of leukemia that is, unfortunately, not one that is easy to treat. He was a wonderful person and I feel very fortunate to have known him. He certainly leaves a wonderful legacy with his family. I do get to see Lorraine occasionally, but not as often as I would like. We do try to keep in touch by phone, however, and try to go to as many quilt shows together as we can.

Lorraine with Leslie and Jim

Luanne (3), Laurie (5)

We were very fortunate in Pleasanton to have good and fun neighbors. The Davids, Frank and Betty, and children Robert and Pamela, moved in when we did, and the backyard fences of the subdivision weren't built yet. We became good friends and when the back fence was built, we decided to put a gate between the two yards. They eventually put a swimming pool in so it was a treat to visit them. We spent many evenings having dinner together and lots of laughs. They were like an aunt and uncle to our girls. Our other neighbors, the Harrises, the Boyers, the Pillows, and the Hansons, also were great. We had some progressive dinners around the holidays that united our friendship. As Evelyn Boyer gave a baby shower for Laurie, Betty Pillow gave one for Luanne. Carol Hanson, a nurse, was always helpful in many situations. Through the years, changes have occurred with moves and deaths, and none of the original neighborhood remains.

The spring before Laurie started school, when she was about five, and Luanne, three, we decided to take a five week trip to the East. George and Cris were living in Minneapolis at the time. With our station wagon well loaded we took off going up through Idaho and to Yellowstone National Park through South Dakota, Flintstone Village, Mount Rushmore(Face Mountain to the girls) to Minneapolis. It was a fun trip. We were able to let the girls play and sleep in the back of the car. Seatbelts were not a requirement then. So we would picnic in a park for lunch and let the girls play. Then they would be ready to nap for awhile while we motored on. I had made each one a bean bag seat that was perfect for them. It wasn't crowded at that time in Yellowstone, so we really got to enjoy it all. The girls got to see a bear on a snow bank at one point. They loved Flintstone Village in South Dakota which had replicas of the Flintstone cars and houses. Mt. Rushmore, was quite an awesome thing to see both up close and from a distance.

After visiting with their 'big brother' in Minneapolis we came back through Illinois to visit my Aunt Grace and family. The girls loved catching tree frogs there and this is where we discovered Luanne's love of horses as she fearlessly wandered out and petted and rode my Uncle Art's horses. On the way back to California we took the girls to Disneyland. They were at a fun age to enjoy the costumed characters and the many rides and adventures offered.

That fall Laurie started kindergarten, so that was a fun time to be a parent rather than a teacher. I enjoyed making clothes for the girls and Halloween costumes etc. and they enjoyed wearing the things I made. We took weekends now and then to visit the grandparents in Santa Cruz. They loved to go to the beach. On one of our trips to visit Mom and Dad they surprised us with a family heirloom. The two of them had built a grandfather clock for us and presented it to us. They had built a grandmother clock for themselves, and decided they wanted to make us one. What a treasure that is! I think of them every time I wind it.

Having fun with the Caufield children

A camping trip to Death Valley

When the girls were about seven and nine we bought a small travel trailer and had some fun trips in it. Santa Cruz was close so we made quite a few weekend trips to Cotillian Gardens, a favorite campground. We also did a trip to Columbia in the Gold Country. A fun and memorable time was a trip to Death Valley with the Caufield family. It was during Easter week vacation and we traveled down the highway from Reno, coming along the backside of Yosemite. The first evening we found a place to pull off, have dinner, and spend the night, before venturing on the following morning. As luck would have it, poor Ron got stuck in the mud and had to be pulled out the following day. That night it had snowed, and was beautiful the next morning. Of course, the children all wanted to play in the snow, but we didn't have warm clothing for them. After all we were on our way to Death Valley. Ron worked with George at General Motors and we have always enjoyed their company. Another place we ventured to with them was Fort Bragg to a beautiful campground with wooded sites but within an easy walk to the beach, with many great tide pools. The Caufield boys, Mark and David, and daughter, JulieAnn were about the ages of our girls.

As the girls were growing George and I were attending some social festivities with the Shrine organization in Pleasanton. George was a thirty-second degree mason and had joined the Shrine before we met and I knew he was paying dues yearly to this organization but was not very active. A school secretary at Alisal School in Pleasanton where I had taught sat with us at a school dinner one night and her husband was active in the Shrine Patrol, one of the marching units in parades, and he invited George to come to one of the meetings. So soon after attending, George became a 'patrolman'. There were many fun activities and we met many nice people through this affiliation. We enjoyed doing a lot of decorating and coming up with ideas for the different social functions. I also had made George a Santa suit and he enjoyed using it every opportunity he got. He became more active in the Masonic lodge. It was during these years that we were privileged to go to Hawaii for a convention with a group of other Shriners. Our first trip to Hawaii was a wonderful adventure. At that time I remember thinking I would love to bring the girls here someday. Mom kept the girls on our trip and they loved getting to visit Grandma and Grandpa. On some of the other overnight excursions we took, the girl's Aunt Inger would watch them. We had some good little baby-sitters in our neighborhood, Beth Boyer, Susan Pillow, and Debbie Raglund, that also would help us out on occasion. I don't remember Mema, George's mom, babysitting the girls, but they got to enjoy her when she came to visit, and on many Christmas parties at her house with all the cousins and relatives. It wasn't long before they were as tall as she, as she was only about four feet, ten inches tall.

We would visit George's mom and stepfather, Tony on occasion in Hayward and enjoy their beautiful yard. We spent usually the Sundays before Christmas there for George's relatives Christmas annual party. George would often play Santa Claus until the little ones became older and wise enough to recognize his watch, ring and voice. It was always a fun occasion and the cousins got a chance to play together. Mema was a perky little gal that had energy enough to do many things, digging in her garden, doing income taxes for people well into the age of ninety-three, and hating to have to give it up for health reasons. She had an interest in people and was curious about many things. We lost her when she was ninety-three due to a faulty heart valve that she chose not to replace. Her husband, Tony, followed her shortly after her death. I miss those times as I miss George's youngest sister, Inger, who was always a lot of fun. Living in San Jose, she was a fun person to visit, and interested in sewing and decorating as I am. We spent some fun times in the fabric stores. She passed away in 2007 of cancer at the age of seventy-three. Her children, Richard, Maurine, Bobby and Judy and her many grandchildren will carry on her legacy. George's other sister, Phyllis, lives about two hours away as does Kathy, her daughter, and Patrick, her son. Robert, Phyllis's other son lives in Alameda. Viggo, another brother of George's, lives in San Bernardino. He lost a wonderful wife, Jan, in 2007 also. That year was quite a year for us. His children, Lisa and Erick, live in the Sacramento area. He also has step-children and grandchildren scattered in the northwest. He now enjoys his two little Chihuahuas, Buttons and Happy. George's youngest brother, Nils, Inger's twin, lives in Idaho.

George didn't know his birth father until he was forty-two. We had returned from our five-week vacation east and received a letter in the mail. It was from a George Bernard Darr. In reading it George discovered his father had lived in Marysville, California for many years. He had been involved in police work, which is something George had always been interested in. He had remarried after divorcing George's mom and had another son, Aleck. Aleck had tracked down George through the Department of Motor Vehicles, having worked there. So George got to meet his father, which is someone he had often wondered about. George Bernard, Aleck and his wife Nancy, also came down to Pleasanton and we enjoyed getting to know them and seeing resemblances in them. About one and a half years after that George Bernard passed away of a heart attack. Alec and Nancy still live in Sacramento. George was able to connect with George B.'s brother, his Uncle Ralph, a delightful man. We traveled to Eastern Oregon to spend some time with him.

George Bernard, George Gregory and Aleck Darr

After Luanne started school I thought perhaps I could sell Avon as a little side line. I enjoyed meeting a lot of people and talking with adults, however, when I didn't quite make it home by the time Luanne got out of school, she would come looking for me, so I decided to give it up.

When Laurie was about seven and Luanne, five, another major event happened in my life. I received a call about three o'clock one morning from Mom. Dad had passed away in the night of an apparent heart attack at the age of seventy seven. He had been diagnosed about three years earlier with congestive heart failure. He had also, about that time, been diagnosed with bladder cancer and during other exams discovered he had leukemia. At that time he had spent about two weeks in the hospital. Until that time Dad had never been sick during my childhood. This seemed like a lot all at once. He had been a cigarette smoker all his life and unfortunately it had taken a toll on him. About six to eight months before his death he stated he did not want to return to that hospital, and he did try to quit the smoking habit but was just unable to. Losing my dad left a void in my life as I always felt his strong love for all of us even though he had difficulty expressing it.

I know Mom did a lot of retrospective thinking after Dad's passing. One of her main regrets was that Dad and Ted's relationship was not the best and she wished she could have done more to fix it. Remember, Mom was a fix-it person.

As I had mentioned earlier my dad had come from Tennessee on suggestion of his brother. Coming from a large family Dad was the youngest and last of his family. He never went back to visit but thought of them probably more than we know. He would often send back boxes of oranges to them at Christmas time. He had a great respect for people, especially women and mothers. He once said he thought a wife and mother had the hardest job of anyone. I never once heard him utter a swear word and he was often turned off by some of the risqué behavior being shown on television. The brother that had brought him to California ended up returning to Tennessee and he and his wife, Pearl, had nine children, two girls and seven boys. Wanting to meet these cousins, Mom and I took a trip to Nashville that was a wonderful experience. We met these great caring soft-spoken families and learned more about the Gaws. I got to visit the place where my dad grew up as a small child in the "hollers of Tennessee." He used to tell me that if you laid flat on your back at noon you might see the sun, but the high hills kept things pretty secluded. I also began to understand why he chose California and wasn't too anxious to return to those "hollers". I do wish he could have visited his nephews and nieces, however, to see what wonderful people they were.

George and I took a trip back again with the girls and had a beautiful visit. I saw in one of my cousins, Lloyd, an astounding resemblance to my dad. During one of our get-togethers, as all the children were downstairs playing in the rumpus room, and the grown-ups were upstairs talking, I was amazed at this resemblance. Pretty soon Laurie came upstairs and I just asked her, "Laurie, who does Lloyd remind you of?" She immediately said, "Grandpa". So it wasn't just my wishful thinking. Although I don't get to see my Tennessee relatives much, they really hold a special place in my heart.

My grandma eventually moved in with Mom after Mom sold the four-plex and bought a mobile home. Mom did take some nice trips, one to Europe to Oberamagua, to see the Passion Play, a performance depicting the life of Christ, that is done every ten years. She also got to see some other sites in Europe. She took a trip to Ireland, too, that she really enjoyed. I am so glad she was able to do these things. She kept a lot of fond memories of these trips including some of a very cordial and fun Irishman in an Irish pub that paid her some special attention.

Mom took Grandma to see the Rose Parade in Pasadena one New Years' Day. I recently thought of how much they said they enjoyed it so much. I was recently able to take a bus trip there with my friends Nancy and Roberta. It was a very special time other than the fact that I did not feel the best overcoming a sinus problem, and Nancy became ill while we were there.

About two and a half years following my dad's death we lost my grandma who suffered from first a massive heart attack, and then surgery to repair a blood clot in her leg that was unsuccessful. Grandma was a wonderful grandma and played a big part in my life, another person I really miss. Now another tragedy to deal with, Mom ended up selling her mobile home and moving into a condominium in Santa Cruz. She used to say that whenever there was a crisis in her life, she had to make changes, and she didn't wait long to make them.

Easter in Santa. Cruz with Grandmother (Gigi)

Laurie and Luanne were both campfire girls and did a lot of fun activities with their respective groups. I became a co-leader with my neighbor, Lynda Clough, and we did some fun things with the girls. They were a great little group and gave us some challenges along the way. After doing a little substitute teaching, I secured a teaching position at a Christian School in Dublin when the girls were about eleven and thirteen. I interviewed for a sixth grade position and received the offer. I was a little unsure of the age group at the time since my experience had been with first and second graders. However, in talking with the current sixth grade teacher and knowing the class would only consist of eighteen students I took it. It was a wonderful group of students. I really enjoyed the age and saw a lot of growth, physical, social, and scholastic, within the year. I continued that position for five more years.

Because of George's lodge affiliations he was involved as a "Rainbow Dad" and worked with the local Rainbow chapter of girls. So when our girls reached the age of thirteen we thought they would like to join one of the Masonic youth groups, the Rainbow Girls, or the Jobs Daughters. We took them to an installation for each group so they could decide if they would like to be a part of this. They both chose Jobs Daughters. Perhaps it was the white robes they wore as opposed to formals. They both joined when they became thirteen and had some good experiences with the group including some conventions and some of those close enough to Disneyland to enjoy trips to that adventureland as well. I became director of music, a much needed fill, and worked with the girls and enjoyed the job for about three and a half years.

It was at a Jobs-Rainbow-Demolay(for boys) dance where Luanne met Brett Cunningham, her to be husband. He was involved in Demolay, as was his father, David, and they attended many social functions together.

During the third year I was teaching we started experiencing problems with our older daughter, Laurie. She had become a rather strong-willed child and was having some social difficulties in school. As a result she had picked some friends that were not too great of an influence on her. She began to skip school, often not realized by us until conference time, slipping out at nights and having some problems causing a lot of turmoil. At the same time my brother, Ted, now living in Florida, was suffering from cancer, and I was concerned and wanted to go back to visit him. I had gone back with Mom to Bethesda, Maryland, to the National Institutes of Health when he had undergone lung surgery, but felt I needed to see him at this time as his prognosis wasn't good. Mom had supported Ted from the very beginning of his cancer diagnosis as I mentioned earlier. When I went back he had realized at that point that his days were numbered, and I also realized that fact of life. About a month after I returned home he passed away.

We continued to struggle with Laurie, seeking counseling and trying to fix the problems. The police became involved a couple of times and she became unmanageable at home. Regretfully, she was made a ward of the court and ordered to finish school in a special place in northern California. This was a very difficult thing for us to endure. We were able to visit hera couple of times and corresponded to her and she did graduate from the school along with about eight others. We feel she missed out on some special school events but at the time that was the only answer to the problem.

Thelma's retirement

Thelma and Boss William Murphy

Luanne missed having her sister around but seemed to understand the problem. In the meantime Luanne continued to enjoy Jobs and Brett. It seems that one of the policemen that dealt with Laurie had a son in my class at school. He chose to share the information about Laurie with the principal at my school, and I was not given a contract for the following year. I guess they felt a Christian School shouldn't have a faculty member with family problems. Although that was never discussed, I feel that was the reason for the termination. I had also had to reprimand one of my students quite often who happened to be a son of a board member.

There was a time when Mom was in the condo that I tried for a couple of days to contact her by phone with no success. I became quite concerned, and George and I drove down one night, about one and a half hours away, to check on her. Her car was gone so we just assumed she went somewhere but didn't know where. We left a note and she called within a couple of days as we still worried. She had been staying with a lady from her church that had surgery and was helping her. It was shortly after that time when we convinced her to move closer. So she got an apartment in Pleasanton. One of the first things I remember that happened shortly after her move was her cataract surgery, and I was glad she was close enough to be able to help. She was also diagnosed with macular degeneration at that time. Shortly after her move we found out about Ted's diagnosis of cancer. Mom's caring nature and concern led to her going back to stay with Ted and help in any way she could. At that time Ted and Bonnie had divorced and there was another lady, Betty in Ted's life. I know that Mom wanted to help in her way that she always was known for but in retrospect it was a very difficult time for her. As she lived each day with my brother's illness, it seemed there was a competitiveness in the house between her and Betty as they cared for Ted. She was a comfort to Kim and David as they were not able to be with their dad all the time. Ted passed away at the age of forty eight on September 17th, the anniversary of my parent's marriage. Unfortunately, there were hard feelings after Ted's passing due to some selfish gestures on Betty's part, and her inconsideration for David and Kim. Mom brought Ted to California to be buried with his father in Santa Cruz which seemed quite bittersweet. It was so difficult to lose my big brother. His children are very dear to me and I'm so sad he didn't get to be a part of his grandchildren's lives. I see him in David and Kim, and also in Ryan, Kim's son. I know I will continue to enjoy some of the same traits as I watch them through the years. I'm sure he's just enjoying them from a different perspective.

Mom was exhausted following the ordeal she had been through and she began questioning where she lives. I happened to say one day, "Mom, I wish we had a little apartment here for you". And she said, "That sounds so good." We started and planning and that ended up being the beginning of a new beginning.

After much discussing and planning we decided to remodel and add an upstairs apartment for Mom. We found a contractor to do the work and he produced a very nice apartment for Mom that she loved. We also enlarged our family room due to the stairs and later added a new deck and outside entrance from Mom's apartment to the yard. It was during these years that she often invited her little lady friends from church to come over following church for lunch and or a game of Rumikub. What a delightful group these little ladies were. We celebrated Mom's eightieth birthday with a big surprise party for her that was a very fun time. It was wonderful to be able to just run up the stairs and visit with Mom. We loved so many of the same things and we could always understand and enjoy one another. Mom was quite a political spirit and loved watching CNN and the political programs. She would get excited over the elections and new congressmen. She was a democrat and often became very upset during different issues. She used to quote my dad's saying, "They were a democrat until they got their bellies full, then they turned into a republican".

Thelma dancing with Brother Gill

Mom and Grandma

A family vacation to Hawaii, mom, me George,
Stephanie, David, Ryan, Kim, Ed

George had worked thirty-two years for General Motors when they began downsizing and changing the plant over to the NUMMI(new united motors manufacturers, Inc.) and merging with Toyota. They offered either early retirement or relocation to an eastern or mid-western plant. The girls were pre-teens and established in school and we questioned uprooting and moving them. So George opted for an early retirement and we stayed in Pleasanton. He felt he needed something so he took a job with a pest control company for awhile and then began working with Ken Shively, a Shrine friend, doing tile-work. When Ken retired and his son took over the business, George began working for a Courier Co. and he drove all over, many miles a day, a tiring job. The day of the San Francisco and Bay Area earthquake, he was close to the section that collapsed. I didn't know where he was until eight o'clock that night. I often worried about him driving so much.

I guess Mom and I inherited Grandma's dreaming spirit in a sense. I can remember planning with Mom how fun it would be to start our own restaurant making something like soul food, like chicken & dumplings, or chili, or beans & rice, and other wonderful comfort foods that we felt pretty confident about making. I can remember one time planning to start our own Lingerie business, selling it on a home plan business, something like Tupperware, and other home parties. We both made up some fancy lingerie, but didn't get much farther than that. Our marketing skills were not too good, and we needed lots of help. I think all the lingerie went as gifts to some people or were handed over to the cancer society for their clothing benefits.

Kim, Ted's daughter, who had completed her business degree in Boston had taken a position in a bank in Boston and Mom and I made a trip to visit her one year at the end of April. I hadn't been to Boston before so it was quite an adventure. When we flew into Logan Airport it was snowing quite heavily. Kim picked us up and we stayed in her small Beacon Hill apartment where the brick buildings have so much character. The next day we walked all over, and I'll never forget seeing the tulips peeking out of the snow at Boston Common. I was very impressed with Boston and couldn't wait to return. Well, I got that opportunity when Kim became engaged to Ed McLaughlin, and Mom and I again went back for their wedding. The wedding was held in Andover, New Hampshire, and the reception was held in the social hall and dining room of Ragged Mountain hunting and fishing club where Bonnie and her husband, Dick, lived. It was a pretty little wedding and so much fun meeting Ed's family at the rehearsal dinner, and getting more acquainted with Stephanie Bzdek, David's fiancée. It was another memory-making time.

It was the end of September when we returned and time to start the finishing touches for Luanne's wedding which was coming up on November 7th.

Luanne got a part-time job when she was a Jr. working in an office and then one at the local movie theater and on graduating another for a different company. Brett formally proposed to Luanne on bended knee at Marie Callendar's restaurant (caught on film by David, Brett's dad.) We gave them an engagement party in our back yard which was a fun event. Plans were made for a November wedding. It worked out that they were married one week before our thirtieth anniversary. She found a dress she loved, made plans for décor, and other things she wanted. I got to make the bridesmaid dresses which were in four jewel tones, coral, emerald, sapphire, and purple. She gave out personalized Christmas ornaments for favors. Lesley, Brett's mother, help decorate some of the pretty baskets for the tables in which to put the ornaments. Lesley and David hosted a wonderful rehearsal dinner, and It was a great event, with the wedding ceremony at the John Knox Presbyterian Church in Dublin, and the reception in San Ramon at the community center. Our baby had grown up. They honeymooned in Hawaii, and returned with the sad news that David, Brett's dad, had died suddenly one week after the wedding. A very loved man, especially with the youth groups, would greatly be missed.

About a year later David and Stephanie tied the knot at a secluded little winery in Northern California inland from the ocean off of Sea Ranch, a community of beach houses. It was a fun weekend with the rehearsal dinner on Friday night, wedding Saturday evening, and dancing into the night outdoors, then a brunch on Sunday morning. Mom now had the satisfaction of knowing another grandchild was settled and she was happy about that.

Another one of those telepathic moments hit me one day when I was upstairs chatting with Mom. We both felt that we would probably be hearing about the planning of a baby with Ed and Kim before too long. I happened to say, "I think I'll go get some yarn and start knitting something." About that time the phone rang, and it was Kim calling to share the news that she was pregnant. Well, I did go and get some yarn and knitted a two-piece baby outfit in red since we knew the baby (sex unknown) would be born in October. It would have a Christmas outfit. Ryan Michael arrived October 18th and has been a big spark in his and our family. The first time I got to meet him was when he was about four months old. Kim was working for a travel agency, and was going to be hiring some tour guides in San Diego. Mom and I flew down and met her and Ryan in San Diego at the airport, stayed in the hotel with her and babysat Ryan while she did her thing. Ryan was joined about two years later be a baby sister, Hannah Nicole. Again, a trip to Boston was planned to see Hannah and witness the baptism of both these little dolls. Now they all live in Marblehead, Massachusetts, a beautiful area, and are experiencing life close to the ocean. Ed is an attorney in Boston, and Kim is a consultant for a travel company, and Ryan and Hannah are experiencing their teen years.

David and Stephanie had purchased a home in San Rafael which was like a tree-house. It was all windows on one side with surrounding trees to afford privacy and had a wonderful deck with a view of the San Rafael Bridge. David had his own computer company and Stephanie worked for a pharmaceutical company. They were also making plans for a family. We were excited when they welcomed little Anna Caroline on Sept 4th into their family. We made trips north to visit and they visited us in Scotts Valley when we moved there. Anna was joined by a sibling, Gabrielle Therese, born about two years later on Mar 22nd.

Mom and Hannah in her christening dress

Prior to Gabrielle's birth Mom and I had been to see her brother, Clay in the Veteran's hospital in San Francisco and just decided since we were close, we would run up to San Rafael to see Dave and Steph. We called ahead to see if they were home, o.k. etc. and according to Stephanie all was good. So we got there, and found out that Steph had been in labor all day. David was just getting home, went in and fixed dinner for all of us. We sat and ate, and finally Stephanie said, "I think we need to go, David". I'm sure she was in much more discomfort than she wanted to appear. She was also very thorough in telling me what to do if there were problems with Anna, "Call this babysitter" or these others or just, "Bring her to us." They finally left. About an hour later David called, "I guess it's a good thing we didn't stay for dessert. We have another little girl." As I was sitting with Anna on the couch that evening reading her a story, she all of a sudden said, "The baby just popped out." It was probably about the time her sister did just pop into the world. It just shows how strong our thought waves, probably from Stephanie and David. can be. The two beautiful little blonds and their parents now live in Golden, Colorado close to some of Stephanie's family, and where David can take them fishing and have lots of outdoor adventures with them.

After being married for about eight months Brett and Luanne decided to move to Utah, on advice from a friend who had moved or lived there. We hated to see them go so far away but had to "give them wings". George helped them move and I'm sure had difficulty leaving them so far away.

After completing her GED, Laurie wanted to pursue some art studies and took some classes at the local Jr. College. She took a trip to London to study Shakespeare and came back geared up even more for the theater. She later enrolled in San Francisco State for some classes. Unfortunately, an earthquake occurred while she was living on the fourteenth floor and scared her to the point she didn't wish to return. She remained in San Francisco, however, to work and experience city life and loved it. It was here where she met Lawrence, whom she loved and they became roommates. They enjoyed the same thing and did so many things together. A devastating thing happened after they shared about eleven years together when he suffered a heart attack and complications during heart surgery and passed away. Unfortunately this happened very close to Christmas and each year during the holidays results in a sad time for Laurie.

People often ask questions to adoptive parents regarding the process. For us it was a great time to be able to have these two little wonderful people in our lives. I could not have felt they were anymore mine than

I felt when we went though the whole process of adoption. Of course, I felt it was a little more final when they were legally ours, about one year after bringing them home. They were a joy and I felt quite full-filled in my motherhood roles. They played together well as children but are very different just as birth sisters can be. Laurie entertained herself quite well, as Luanne enjoyed being around others more. Laurie was often more serious about things where Luanne tended to be more happy-go-lucky. They were quite challenging, but seeing them grow and become individuals in their own right has been fun and enlightening. I cannot imagine loving them any more than I do and I am so thankful for them. They are SO SPECIAL! I know that George feels the same way too.

When you adopt a child there are times when you wish you had a one-way mirror to see where that little being came from. Who does she get her gorgeous eyes from, or the sunny disposition? Well, we got that opportunity as did our girls. I feel every being has a curiosity about their ancestry. I know after meeting my paternal cousins for the first time, I felt that bond immensely.

When Laurie was twenty she wrote a letter to Children's Home Society to inquire about her birth parents. They notified her that her birth mother had written them when she was eighteen and expressed an interest that if Laurie was ever interested she would be likewise. So in this way they were connected. I remember how excited Laurie was at the time. Andre, her birth mother, met her in San Francisco where Laurie was living at the time. That was when Laurie discovered her birth parents eventually married, had two more boys and one other girl, so Laurie had one full-blood sister and two brothers. She met them all and they all celebrated her twenty-first birthday with us. I got to see that Laurie was a combination of the two and received her beauty from the best of both of them. Unfortunately, after establishing a relationship with them, there was a big misunderstanding between Laurie and her birth parents and the relationship did not last. I do hope at some point they can enjoy each other again.

Before Luanne had children and during her residence in Utah she was experiencing asthma as she did in her teens. The doctor would ask about her background and she would have to say, "I don't know. I'm adopted". Well, she. Like Laurie, contacted Children's Home Society and luckily her birth mom had written a similar letter, so Peggy flew to Utah and met Luanne. Yes, Luanne's grandfather suffered a lot from asthma and Luanne found out about her background. Although her birth parents never married, they were still somewhat in touch with one another. Luanne has two half-sisters from Peggy that she has met and continues to remain on good terms with. She was able to meet her birth father, David, who lives in Alaska, a couple of years ago in Arizona at his son's wedding. They had corresponded prior but seeing him face-to-face was a good thing. She has two half brothers from David. Luanne was able to get to know her birth mom's parents and found she "clicked, and loved her grandfather. I also got to share in that friendship. Both of those grandparents have passed and I'm glad we got to know them.

The Darr Family

The year following my termination with the Christian School, I took a position with a private school as a teacher for a combination first and second grade. It was a small k-3 school with nice classrooms. I enjoyed the children, but in January of that year I fell on some ice in front of our house and broke my right wrist. Fortunately, I am ambidextrous to some extent and was able to do a lot with my left hand. The position only lasted for one year. They wanted me to do a kindergarten class the following year, but I turned it down because I felt the students were too young and I questioned myself about it.

I then began working for Huntington Learning Center, a center that helps build skills for all ages, even adults on a one-to-one basis. I really enjoyed that, met some wonderful people, and especially enjoyed helping an adult lady learn to read. It wasn't full time, being hourly, but quite satisfying. Would you believe that the following year I slipped at home on the same spot and broke my left wrist? It took a good nine weeks for it to heal. But it was much easier tutoring on a personal basis than trying to manage a classroom with a broken bone. After I began working for the center I also took on the job of setting up a tutoring center for preschool and daycare in Pittsburg, California. That was a great experience and I loved what I did, everything from writing grants to physically setting up the center to working with the children. I did get it all going and ready for someone to take it over as I just was too stressed with the long distance drive and congestion through Walnut Creek and Highway Four at the busiest times of day. It led to a fender bender for me one day on the way home and I gave it up, and went back to working only locally for the center. I stayed with the center until we retired and moved from Pleasanton.

While I was working at the Huntington Learning Center, I got an opportunity to see New York City. I was sent to Tenafly, New Jersey for some training. I left on a Friday for training sessions the following Monday. I was told there would be a limousine waiting for me at the airport. I thought I've never had the opportunity to ride in a limo, great! Well, when I arrived a man was standing holding a sign with my name on it. As I accompanied him, he apologized about the limo breaking down, and instead we boarded a van, the noisiest one I've ever been in. After arriving at the hotel I walked into my room. There I was all by myself. My counterpart from Walnut Creek wasn't coming in until Sunday. When I awoke on Saturday morning, I thought I can either sit around this room for a couple of days, or venture out and see something. Well, I made the decision to take the bus into New York City. After about forty-five minutes on the bus, I arrived at the Port Authority in downtown New York. I look around the huge display of terminals, not knowing where to go. When I had boarded the bus back in Tenafly, in talking to another lady at the bus stop, she had warned me not to ask anyone questions unless they had on a brown uniform. I found the restroom and decided to take advantage of its closeness. There were about three women sleeping on the floor which I assumed was probably, and unfortunately normal. I had carefully tucked some extra money and a credit card inside my bra for some crazy reason, and held on to my purse quite carefully. After the restroom I went to an information booth and asked about tours of the city. She directed me to exit the terminal on eighth street and go down about three blocks to the Gray-line Tours bus lines. So out on a busy street I went. After the first cab wouldn't start, I tried a second one that took me right to the place. Luckily there would be a two hour tour within the next fifteen minutes.

The group was made up of about eighteen people. We drove the main sites of the city as the guide explained each mark. I was quite disappointed with Times Square, however I'm not sure what I was expecting. One stop was above a Buddhist temple that we toured and were able to shop at a little store above it that we were told was legitimate and one with fair prices. I bought a bracelet just to have a souvenir to remember the trip from. The twin towers of the World Trade Center were awesome and I'm so glad I was able to see them. We stopped again at the park overlooking the Statue of Liberty, and that was quite a sight. When we arrived back at the Gray-line Tour office, I decided I would just walk back to the Port Authority. There were many street people lounging around. At the terminal I didn't have to wait long to catch a bus back to Tenafly. I just knew I wanted to get back before dark. I made it, walked into my hotel room, and was relieved, but quite proud of myself, thinking of how I got to see some wonderful things.

On Sunday, Mary, from Walnut Creek came in and she, of course, was anxious to see some things, so on Monday evening after our classes we went into the city for dinner and sight-seeing. We ate near Rockefeller Center, and visited the beautiful St. Patrick's Cathedral. We had a harrowing taxi ride back to the terminal, but at least we were together, and made it back safe and sound. We both wished we could have seen a play in the city, but our time was quite limited.

We loved to go to Santa Cruz, about one and a half hours away, as a get-away. One time on a trip that Mom and I took there we happened to go through Scotts Valley, which is about five miles before you get to Santa Cruz. She mentioned about a lady she knew at the County offices living in a mobile home park there, and as we were looking for it we happened upon another mobile home park, Montevalle. As we drove around in this beautiful, wooded community we fell in love with it. With the big rustic clubhouse built by a big water wheel. and a big pond with ducks and benches to sit and enjoy nature, it was a very pleasant place to be. Located so close to the Santa Cruz beach it was enticing. We also met some very nice people as we inquired about certain things relating to the park.

When we returned home that day we told George about this place we had adventured to, and that weekend we all went to take another look. The more we talked, the more we felt the time had come for George to retire and enjoy life, and kick back a little. We knew it would be a big down-sizing but we were ready. Our house held a lot of wonderful memories and held a special place in our hearts as did the community of Pleasanton which we witnessed grow from about five thousand to fifty thousand and is now much larger. We got our house ready to sell, and kept a watch on available properties in Montevalle. It took about seven to eight months to sell our house. We followed with a garage sale in which David and Stephanie came to help. It was unbelievable the amount of "stuff" we had collected in the thirty-two years we had lived there. We went from a 3200 square foot home and apartment to a 1500 square foot mobile home. It had a special little separate room and bath off the deck so Mom could have her own little space to herself along with a bedroom and bath for her in the main part of the home. It was quite livable, our "little cabin in the woods". There were many trees and shrubs all around us and the weather was wonderful. It would get warm and pleasant during the spring and summer days but we were close enough to the ocean to get the night time cool air. Although a little hilly as Montevalle was in some places, we were pretty flat, with only steps to get in the house and we were fairly close to all the activities at the clubhouse and close by to walk down to get the mail. We all loved it here and met some wonderful people, who had moved there from many places. They, too, had usually downsized from bigger homes and now were satisfied with a different life style. George and I became involved quite soon by becoming the Social Activities Chairmen. We planned dinners, bus trips and other activities for all the residents. By doing this we met almost everyone that lived in Montevalle. I will never forget the fun we had preparing dinners in the big kitchen and working alongside my special friends, Gloria Peterson and Theresa Jacobs, and so many others. I joined a quilting group called the Valley Girls that included women from Scotts Valley, Felton, and Boulder Creek. What a special group of ladies they were. Nancy, our neighbor, was such a fun person. We had many great visits in Scotts Valley from our friends, and relatives and they always loved our abode.

About four years after Brett and Luanne moved to Utah George received a birthday present on his birthday in August, which was a photo frame saying Grandpa on it with a note on it saying he would be one in March. Lesley, Brett's Mom, who also has an August birthday, also got one on the same day. They wanted to make sure we all found out at the same time.

That was exciting! We went back to Utah right before the baby was born and got to be there and see a beautiful little boy the day after he was born at the hospital. That was a VERY SPECIAL MOMENT! Gabriel Will was such a cute baby and is still a big light in our lives.

We visited them again on his first birthday. After the visit we continued from Utah on back to a Fugate family reunion in Missouri and also visited relatives in Tennessee. On our way back to California we stopped again to see Luanne, Brett, and Gabe and received good news, that they decided they were moving back to California so they could all be closer to relatives. What wonderful news that was to us.

In putting out job feelers, Luanne interviewed for a position in Visalia. She flew out at that time and I drove down, met her in Fresno, and spent some time with her. She got the job and they moved out to Visalia. When they moved she was pregnant again. We drove out and helped them move. George and Cris came down from Oregon, and met them here in Visalia and helped a lot with the physical labor involved in moving. Having the family four hours away was much better than fourteen hours.

On August 26th, George's birthday, Grace Elizabeth was born as George and I sat outside the Visalia Hospital taking care of Gabriel. Another memory maker was made and every year we celebrate both of their birthdays on the same day. George calls his granddaughter "His Birthday Present".

While we were living in Scotts Valley, we also took some trips to Davis, California, south of Sacramento. Mom's youngest brother, Clay who was living in Davis, and having health problems, was due to be released from the hospital. We knew he was not able to care for himself so we had him moved to a facility in Santa Cruz so we could help him in any way he needed. From there he improved to the point where he wanted a little place of his own. We found him a nice little apartment with a landlady that lived on the property, and enjoyed having him as a tenant. He did well even though he was wheelchair bound. He had a nice van with a ramp that he could travel in with his chair, so I would often take him places, such as the Veteran's clinic in Monterey or the grocery store, or to pick out something new for his apartment, which he loved to decorate. Clay was a lot of fun and I felt a special bond to him. He called one morning to tell me he didn't feel well and wanted me to come over. He had a high fever and I called the ambulance to take him to the hospital. I sat with him in emergency until he was seen by a doctor and admitted to a room. His immune system was compromised, and he had a bad case of emphysema and had suffered many bouts with pneumonia. I just thought this was another one of those episodes, so I left and came back the next morning. When I went to his room, I found they had moved him to Intensive Care and was unable to see him at that time. I went back home and reported to Mom who was very fragile at that time, having had some health problems herself.

I received a call that afternoon from the doctor that they were trying different meds on Clay but he was very sick. I told the doctor that I didn't know whether to bring my ninety-two year old mother in or not because I was worried about how it would affect her. He advised me it might not be a good idea. He called again early evening to tell me Clay was dying and thought I might want to come. By that time I just told Mom the truth, the doctor was so concerned, that Clay was dying and we needed to go. We did. We got to the hospital and Clay was on life support systems, and they were waiting for our approval to disconnect all machines. It was a VERY difficult time for us but I managed to get through it knowing I had to. Mom did well, too. It seems that God gives you that strength when it is needed. Mom's brother, Curt, had died the previous December and this was the second brother for Mom to lose in such a short time.

We planned a funeral for him where my grandmother, Dad, and Ted are buried. Many friends from Davis came as did relatives from the Bay Area. It just so happened that Billy, Clay's brother, living in Missouri at the time, was on his way to see him right before he died. Although he didn't get to visit him, he was here for the funeral. We all got together at our home after the services, and relived some of Clay's good moments. Unfortunately, Billy passed away about two years later.

I fully believe there are angels, here on earth, that help us in times of need. Shortly after the funeral I had to take care of Clay's possessions. So while my cousin, Lynn, was here she and I went over and held an estate sale at his apartment. We were able to sell many things, but I had to go a second day by myself to finish up. Clay was quite an accomplished musician and great piano player. He had talked about wishing he could find a small piano for his apartment but hadn't reached that point. As I sat on the couch waiting for buyers to show up, a nice friendly man, the first customer, came in and asked, "Do you have a piano?" I was taken by surprise, and said, "He wanted one, but hadn't got around to finding one." He came over and started talking, asking about his passing etc. It so happened that this man was a caregiver for a man in Scotts Valley, and also volunteered at some service organizations throughout Santa Cruz. He turned out to be one of the nicest "angels" I have ever encountered. He stayed there almost all day with me and helped. When one lady came in and got off on a tangent talking about something, I don't remember what at this point, he sensed my confusion, interceded and calmly said something right to rescue the situation. George had stayed home with Mom and later came to see how things were going. The man, Bob, was his name, offered to take some of the things we couldn't sell and didn't wish to keep, to some of the organizations he knew of. He wasn't a bit pushy, but just mentioned he would be glad to do these things for us. The next day when George and I went over to load up the remaining things Bob was there to help him load things into his truck and load other things to take away in his truck. I believe he was sent to help me through a trying time in my life. I ran into Bob about six months later in a supermarket parking lot helping a little old man, perhaps his client.

One of the big events we had while we lived in Montevalle was Mom's 90th birthday party we threw for her. Her sister Grace and her husband and their son, Gary and his wife Evelyn from Kansas flew out, as did Kim and her family. David and family, Luanne and family, Laurie, her brother, Clay, and her nieces and nephew from the Bay Area, Greg and Debbie, from Oregon, George and Cris, also from Oregon, Lorraine, her "other daughter" and many of her long-time friends and also many friends from Montevalle. It was in a great reception hall there and David, Ed, Kim, Cris and I did all the food, just what Mom wanted. It was a wonderful weekend, with celebrations for about four to five days with relatives that had traveled so far to come. I am so glad we were able to show her how much she meant to us.

It was about a year later that Mom began having a few health problems. She had fallen out of bed one night and injured her back again and had to spend some time in a care facility. As they kept her so heavily sedated and confused, I was anxious to get her released and back home. After that her little legs and knees began bothering her and causing much pain. There were many visits to Dr. Motyka whom she loved and who obviously thought Mom was quite the little lady.

As time went by and Luanne and the grandchildren would visit when they could and we would try to get down to see them, we got to see how Visalia was growing and adding new developments. Brett and Luanne were looking for a larger home to also accommodate Brett's mom, Lesley. We would look at models on occasion when we visited. This all began the idea of moving to Visalia, being closer to the family and the possibility of a new and bigger residence. Well, that's what we did. As things proceeded and during the next four years I felt that God orchestrated all the events that occurred. We were all on board for the move including Mom. We had brought her with us to look at the tract of homes we were interested in. Luanne was working for Centex at the time. Many tracts being built had waiting lists and you were put on a six-nine month waiting list if interested. The Centex tract was a little different and Luanne had a bit of an influence with priorities. She lived close and was able to submit our requests and choose our lot which is only about one and a half blocks one way and four blocks if you walk around to her front door from where we live. We were told it would be available for move in on August 1st, 2005. So we had to coordinate our move from Montevalle. We didn't want to have to move twice. So, in consulting Mario, a friend in Montevalle, who was a realtor, we decided to put our home on the market April 1st, 2005. George, in the mean time, had brought about three pick-up loads of things down and put them in storage, partly to stage our place with less furniture, and partly to get an early start.

Well, would you believe that the first couple Mario brought to our home on April 1st wanted it. The man was a contractor who wanted to, along with his wife, find a place to live in Montevalle. He saw some changes he wanted to make but wanted this place. He was also willing to wait until we moved out on July 31st. This was all too good to be true.

So the next months we planned our new home, what we would do, made a trip down to choose options, colors etc. and felt a lot of excitement. Then on July 30th, George brought the last pick-up load down and prepared to be here on the 31st for the phone and cable service order. Mom stayed behind with me as the movers came and I did last minute cleaning. It was a long day. Mom got a permanent that day which spent some time for her and then I had her visit with our neighbor, Theresa, so she could be more comfortable as I did last minute cleaning. We spent the night in Santa Cruz at a motel, both, I think, tired from an emotional and busy day.

When we drove down the next day from Santa Cruz to Visalia we found Brett and Luanne, George, and George and Cris, who had again come from Oregon to help with the move, all helping the movers and putting things away for us. What a blessing to have their help. Cris could organize anything and do it well, and George knows a solution to any problem that you might encounter. They were all such a big help. We had one big problem, however. The new refrigerator they had delivered had a flaw and didn't work so we were living out of ice chests until the new refrigerator arrived.

We settled into our home and it was fun to be in a brand new house and to see our furniture fit nicely as we had planned it. Mom had picked out her bedroom, the one right across from the bathroom. We had a den where she could have her TV and watch what she wanted or she could be alone if she wanted. She often chose to be with us in our great room with livable kitchen, dining and living in one. Then I have a sewing room I can use just for that. The floor plan is very workable and we all love it. We have an extra guest room with twin beds for the grands or other company. Mom used to say, "I just love this house".

George and I took one look at our big back yard and decided to put in a pool. The climate here is extremely hot in the summer, and the pool is something that would get a lot of use. We love it, and so do Gabe and Grace.

The October after we moved into our new home George came down with an illness. After a visit to the dentist that morning he came home to take a nap. I was unable to get him up later and he had no strength whatsoever. I had a wheel chair I had kept that belonged to my Uncle Clay. I called Brett and he helped me get George into the car and I took him to the emergency department at the hospital. That was about 6:00 PM. At 2:00 AM they finally admitted him not knowing yet what the problem was. A couple of days later they diagnosed him with a special strain of pneumonia. He was in the hospital for about 1 and a half weeks.

The following January he had to have prostate surgery. Fortunately, the prostate wasn't malignant, just enlarged. Then in April due to extreme lethargy he was found to have a heart blockage during an angiogram. A four-way bypass was done and then two days following that they needed to operate on his gall-bladder. There was a lot of healing to be done and he was sent to a rehabilitation center for a couple of weeks. He was unable to complete all the therapy due to some other problems. He began to become depressed, not eat, and lose weight. As time progressed he became worse. I thought if I bring him home, feed him home-cooked food, cheer him up by seeing the kids and grandkids, he will improve. I brought him home. He didn't improve. He continued to decline. George and Cris had come for a visit and helped me decide to take him back to the hospital which again was the emergency room. He was highly dehydrated as he wouldn't drink liquids at home either, so they intravenously gave him fluids and tried different kinds of things with him, and tried different antidepressants. Nothing seemed to be working. The last thing the doctor suggested was to insert a feeding tube. I could not make that decision and we got no response from George when asked about it. Since the hospital could do no more for him they suggested palliative care at a local care-giving facility. So I had him moved to Westgate Care Center thinking what else can I do? I remember receiving a call from a Dr. Johnson, a doctor that works with Westgate patients. He talked to me over the phone for a good forty five minutes to an hour. He sounded like a caring patient man and explained what he would do. It was an excruciating time for me. I didn't expect George to return home. I would visit him and he resembled a zombie. His weight got down to 110 and his average weight had been around 190-200 pounds.

Miraculously, George began to improve bit by bit. The doctor had diagnosed him with depression, and dementia, anemia and many other problems. His memory was poor and he would say things that didn't seem to make sense, but day by day he got stronger, gained weight and became a part of the world again. He had different roommates during his stay at Westgate, but I attribute a lot of his successful improvement to John Casarez, one of his special roommates. John is a special person, and a very social being finding things to like about people. He would often talk to George, ask him questions, and he and his wife, Belia, befriended George and me in lots of ways. John left Westgate before George, still has lots of medical problems, but we still keep in touch. I also feel the many prayers said for George by friends and relatives were responsible for his recovery. In time, about two years following his heart surgery George was able to return home. He still has some mobility problems and some health problems, but is a different person much improved from what he was when he entered Westgate.

About six months before George came home Mom was experiencing some confusion, hallucinations, and having more trouble walking etc. She had fallen out of bed a few times, and had a couple of emergency trips to the hospital for low blood sugar. I was back and forth. I found a couple of ladies that stayed with her when I went to see George. Luanne helped as much as she could, and I was so glad to have her close. It was during this time that I felt Mom needed more care than I could physically and mentally give. I couldn't lift her as she needed to be and couldn't leave her alone. So I put her into the Westgate Center where George was. That was another difficult time, to have to leave her at the care center and visit her. She was in a different wing from George, but I got her moved to his wing. His nurses seemed more caring. She would have times that she would start packing things to come home. Those were the hardest times. At other times she had figured out that "everyone at the Care Center was related and it was a family affair." Another time she thanked me for bringing her there. That is the memory I hold on to. There were sometimes I, with Luanne's help, would bring her home to visit, and she got to the point that she was ready to return in the evening.

The last time I brought Mom home was the Christmas Eve before she passed. We took her to the evening services at the church and she got to see Gracie sing with a children's choir. She seemed to enjoy the service. I had decided I would keep her overnight that night. I tucked her in and slept with her. The next morning as I was helping her, she was having a very difficult time with simple tasks, and said, "I just can't do anything anymore." We got through the day going to Luanne's for Christmas brunch. I took her back in the afternoon. I know she enjoyed Christmas but not like the many many times we had all enjoyed it in the past. She was tired and had seen her last Christmas. I feel she also knew that.

Three weeks later when I met with nursing staff at her care-plan meeting, things seemed to be going o.k except she had lost some more weight. In about another week she had started not even getting out of bed and not eating. I remember going in and giving her a kiss like I usually did, and she raised herself up and gave me and big kiss, smiled and lay down. After that she didn't want to eat. The nurses tried to feed her and she balked at food and drink. Then a couple of days later I noticed her trembling was getting worse, and I mentioned to the nurses that she needed some interveinous fluids. They don't give IVs at the center so I had them call the ambulance to take her to the hospital. In the emergency room they ran tests and found out her kidneys were failing. Mom was not responsive at that time and I made a decision between trying dialysis and letting her go, and I chose the latter. I was not going to put her through another painful procedure. I was also not going to send her back to Westgate and experience a painful trip as every time they moved her she cried out in pain. So I opted for a hospice room at the hospital. The doctor thought she might pass that night but she lived another day and a half. She was kept comfortable. She had a wonderful nurse that explained very well what was happening and I couldn't have asked for a more peaceful ending. My last words to her were, "Mom, you can go be a butterfly now". She had often talked about when you die it is like a butterfly coming out of its cocoon and you can just be all around. Mom was a very spiritual person and talked about these things a lot. She was especially a fan of Deepak Chopra's, and had read many of his books. Luanne spent the time with Mom and me and I was so grateful for her company. About the time Mom passed we heard a lullaby from the nursery unit that is played when a new baby is born. That was the only one we had heard while we were there. As life ends, a new one is born.

My wonderful mother

Mom passed on a Sunday. Luanne had called everyone for me. David was at our house by that night and was a big help to me. George and Cris, who had planned on coming to the Bay Area for a class reunion that week anyway, came a little early and helped too. We had a nice service again in Santa Cruz. Mom was laid to rest beside her brother, Clay where she knew she would be. All her grands and great grands were able to come as were her close friends that she worked with when working for the county in Santa Cruz. Marlene, the mother of a family that Mom was a nanny for in Pleasanton was there. Her remaining sister, Grace, and her daughter, Gina, came from Illinois, and her "other daughter", Lorraine, my best friend was there, as were many relatives from the Bay area. We rented a house that weekend in Rio Del Mar with a beautiful ocean view from the deck, and as we sat there reliving episodes in Mom's life we all enjoyed our common love for this beautiful and extraordinary woman.

I believe that events happen in our lives that are times that we are drawn to for various reasons. I certainly have had experiences with "angels" that present themselves at opportune times.

There was one time when Mom was in Westgate that when I visited her she wanted to come home. For some reason she mentioned, "We'll just get a little dog and someone to come in to take care of me and that would be good." I wish it would have been that simple. About two years after Mom passed I was on an errand to Home Depot looking for a part for a chair. It was on a Saturday afternoon. Not finding the part, I thought as I was sitting in the parking lot, I think I will drive over to the shelter to see what dogs they have. George and I had somewhat been talking about getting another Dachshund, on and off again, and sometimes looking in the paper for possibilities. As I drove out to the shelter I questioned myself, but continued to meander on. As I walked into the facilities, in the third kennel from the door, my eyes caught a small, brownish-red dachshund lying on the floor, in with another cute little dog. I thought, "What are you doing here?" I continued on, looking at all the other little creatures waiting for a home. As I was looking at them, one of the volunteers came along, and I just mentioned that I wish I could take them all home. I also asked her about the little dachshund in the first building. She asked, "Would you like to meet him?" I most certainly did, so she took him out of the pen and we took him out into the yard to get a little glimpse of his personality. I fell in love with him. He had just become adoptable that day. I wanted to talk it over with George, so she told the ladies in the office to not take this little dog out to the other facility on Monday, which they sometimes do to expose them to more people. It so happened they were remodeling the other facility so he wouldn't be going out there. It was too late in the day to adopt that day, and they were closed on Sunday, so early on Monday morning George and I went out to see him again. He liked him a lot too, so guess what? We brought him home. I just feel I was led to him, and he has been my constant companion ever since. I feel he is curious about everything I do, and is constantly by my side whenever he can be. We kept the name Doogle, the name the shelter had given him. I had thought we would rename him, but nothing seemed to fit him as well as Doogle. I don't know all his history, but he has adapted well. He was about a year old, they estimated. He loves the grandkids, and most people. It has taken awhile for him to adjust to George, but he is now coming around. We feel he might have been abused by a man or men. He takes to women much more easily.

Since moving to Visalia I have come back close to where I grew up as a child. Being only twenty five miles away from Lemoore, I have enjoyed reconnecting with some close high school friends, Nancy and Roberta. We try to get together as much as we can, sometimes in this area, to lunch and chit-chat, sometimes traveling to Morro Bay where Roberta lives to just be together. They have both lost their husbands, and there have been a lot of happening, but we are still the people we have always been and enjoy life together. We enjoy each other and look forward to our next time together.

I also feel fortunate to have wonderful neighbors on both sides of us. Gary stepped in when George was so ill and helped with yard issues and his uncle, Adam, has mowed and cared for our lawns, doing watering and necessary pruning for us. Gary and his wife, Yvette, are now parents to little Aiden and I can't wait to watch the results. Then Rick and Tiffany are so thoughtful and considerate in so many ways. They are such a good looking family with their three handsome sons, Jose, Michael, and Little Sammy. We are truly blessed by their presence. I was able, along with Tiffany, to help Amanda, another neighbor, make a quilt for her first little one about three years ago. Amanda and Todd welcomed little Noah about two and a half years ago, and are looking forward to another new one in spring.

Laurie, now forty-one, has moved to the Los Angeles area after spending many years in the San Francisco area, and seems to love it. She is still pursuing her love of acting and in the meantime working at different things that are giving her different experiences. I hope she is able to attain her goals and will have a successful life.

Luanne and Brett are raising two wonderful children, Gabriel and Grace. Luanne is an underwriter for a mortgage company and Brett is a land surveyor. Gabriel is a bright, sweet eleven year old with dreams of becoming an engineer. He is interested in how things work and loves to put things together. He also loves the computer, and doing things with it. Grace is another great gal. At nine years of age she loves animals and outdoor life and wishes to be a park ranger. Her compassion and determination are obvious as she does things.

Happy grandchildren, Gabe and Grace

The world is so different today than it was during my childhood. I do feel in many ways there are wonderful advancements, but in some ways there are detriments. I hope my children and grandchildren will realize the improvements and benefits and not have to experience the detriments. I want them to be true to themselves and also be aware of others in the world. Live by that golden rule, "Treat others as you wish to be treated".

The things I value the most in life are things that I feel were passed down to me and some developed from my experiences in life. Music to me is one of God's greatest gifts. I often think of what a void we would have if we didn't have music. It's miraculous how we can arrange a few simple notes and come up with compositions so beautiful and moving to the spirit. How do child prodigies realize these things at such an early age? I feel that music should be in every child's life, and that child should also learn to play music on some instrument of choice. To me it is one of the deeper aspects of life. It demands concentration, discipline, and awards with appreciation and accomplishment. An appreciation of the beauty of nature, the things around us such as the oceans, animals, and a love strong enough to want to preserve all of this is important. One of my favorite places is the Monterey Peninsula, where there is SO much beauty in Big Sur, Pacific Grove, and Carmel, and wonder of life at the Monterey aquarium. You can't give a child too much interest in this area.

I also hope with the computer age in full swing that books do not become more obsolete. There is something about having a good book in hand, and the feeling you can read it as often as you like, which is something special. I also hope that texting by cell-phone does not replace the great conversations people have face-to-face.

Perhaps it was my teaching career that gave me such a love for children and people. Each one is so unique and has so much to offer. I often wonder how the lives of all my students played out, as they each had their specific individual talents and spirits. I feel blessed to have been able to be a part of so many lives. I feel we are products of our environment and also definitely are genetically pre-disposed for certain things. I see both my mother and my father in myself, and yet I have developed some features of my personality from the way I have lived my life. As I age I find myself developing my mom's political interests and find myself watching CNN more and more. I feel Mom in myself so many times and there are times when I see my dad in myself. I have some of the same food loves my dad had, and have some other characteristics like him. I also sense I have some of the same loves and characteristics of my Aunt Grace. It's interesting how those genes are passed on and how they can rearrange themselves to cause different results. It's fun to see my grandchildren with characteristics taken from each of their parents and how amazing these things are as they grow.

I guess my greatest wish is for all the children and people of the world to come to a mutual respect for each other and understanding of why different people are unique. I have always tried to look for and usually seen the good qualities of a person. I feel if we try to look for the common threads between someone else and ourselves, life will be a lot more enjoyable. I do feel hope for our world when I watch such things as the Olympics and see how we all want the same thing basically and we are all so alike in so many ways. We just need to rid the prejudice and exchange it for understanding. We need to hold on to humor and be able to laugh (appropriately) to lift the spirit. We also need to be able to love and be loved in return, something I have certainly had fulfilled in my life.

George and I are now happy in our Glendale St. home. It is good to be at a time in your life where you can sit and reflect on the many treasures of your life. At the same time you know that those earthly treasures are going to diminish and you can't go back to redo or change things you wish you could. You are born with one life and the choice is yours as to how you play it out. Rather than a twenty year old planning out his life, we live each day one at a time, and venture out on something if the mood strikes us. We enjoy the simple things in life, a non-stressing schedule, time for a newspaper in the morning with our cup of coffee, a jump and exercise regiment in the pool, playing solitaire or games or sending and receiving e-mail and information on the computer, petting the dog as he sits in your lap, planning and working on a new quilt, reading a good book, watching a good movie or program on TV, playing games with the grandchildren, having dinner with the whole family. These are all joys of living. I have had a wonderful life being blessed with many things. I suppose many, maybe most people would say this, but I really feel it.

When I reflect and I feel I might have done something differently, I feel, there are reasons for everything that happens in life. My father celebrated seventy seven years, my mother, ninety five years, my brother, only forty eight years. I don't know how many years I will have, but I am grateful for the seventy one years I have been given, and look forward to what our Great Creator has in store for me.

A MOTHER'S NIGHT BEFORE CHRISTMAS
By: Thelma Gaw

Twas the night before Christmas,
I was getting quite frantic and rushing
around in my usual panic.
I had gifts to wrap and cookies to bake,
and if there was time, I would bake a big cake.

After I finished my baking and stuff,
At least, I hoped it would be enough.
I sat down to view the beautiful tree
and wondered if Santa had something for me.

I tucked the two older ones into their beds
with visions of Santa Claus in their wee heads.
I thought of old Santa, I could be jolly too
if I didn't have all this leg work to do.

Just about then I heard such a clatter.
I rushed into the kitchen to see what was the matter.
My youngest was standing there, up on a chair.
All I could do was stand there and stare.

I took one look at his little red belly,
and recognized most of my cranberry jelly.
Just as he reached his hand in for more,
the whole bowl came crashing down to the floor.

I bathed him again and put him to bed,
told him of Santa, a story was read.
I might even say I was proud of myself.
I never did spank the dear little elf.

Just as I started to clean up the floor,
I thought I heard someone knock at the door.
The front door flew open and so did my mouth.
There stood my brother and his wife from the South.

I guess he noticed the shock in my eyes.
He said he wanted their visit to be a surprise.
I fixed them a drink, it was the least I could do.
As a matter of fact, I needed one, too!

Then I picked up their luggage and grabbed me a broom,
and started off toward that awful guest room.
There were papers and boxes, I couldn't begin
to tell of the horrible mess it was in.

Instead of just standing there shaking my head,
I calmly shoved everything under the bed.
When I was through it looked very neat.
I could have thrown both of them out on the street.

When all was finally still in the house,
and nothing was moving, not even a mouse,
I had finally gotten what had to be done,
and decided Christmas really was fun.

ABOUT THE AUTHOR

Nancy Ann Darr was born in Hanford, California, and spent her early years in Lemoore, CA. She is a graduate of the College of Sequoias in Visalia, CA and of Fresno State College in California.

She taught in Mt. Eden School District in Hayward, CA, and in Pleasanton, CA, and Dublin, CA.

She is now retired and living again in Visalia in the San Joaquin Valley with her husband George and is close to her daughter Luanne and grandchildren, Gabriel and Grace.

Get Published, Inc!
Thorofare, NJ 08086
15 April, 2010
BA2010105